D0821194

LADY CHATTERLEY'S LOVER

Loss and Hope

TWAYNE'S MASTERWORK STUDIES

Robert Lecker, General Editor

LADY CHATTERLEY'S LOVER

LOVER

Loss and Hope

ARackel
1998

William K. Buckley

TWAYNE PUBLISHERS • NEW YORK
Maxwell Macmillan Canada • *Toronto*
Maxwell Macmillan International • *New York Oxford Singapore Sydney*

Twayne's Masterwork Studies No. 123

Twayne Publishers   Maxwell Macmillan Canada, Inc.
Macmillan Publishing Company   1200 Eglinton Avenue East
866 Third Avenue   Suite 200
New York, New York 10022   Don Mills, Ontario M3C 3N1

Library of Congress Cataloging-in-Publication Data
Buckley, William K., 1946–
        Lady Chatterley's lover : loss and hope / William Buckley.
                p.   cm. — (Twayne's masterwork studies ; no. 123)
        Includes bibliographical references and index.
        ISBN 0-8057-9432-8 (hard). — ISBN 0-8057-8599-X (soft)
        1. Lawrence, D. H. (David Herbert), 1885–1930. Lady Chatterley's lover.
I. Title. II. Series.
PR6023.A93L215 1993
823'.912—dc20   93-7658
                                                                  CIP

The paper used in this publication meets the minimum requirements of American
National Standard for Information Sciences—Permanence of Paper for Printed Library
Materials, ANSI Z39.48-1984.∞ ™

10 9 8 7 6 5 4 3 2 1 (alk. paper)
10 9 8 7 6 5 4 3 2 1 (pbk.: alk. paper)

Printed in the United States of America.

For
my students

Contents

D. H. Lawrence, Florence, 1928. At the Orioli bookstore. © Robert H. Davis Estate. Reprinted with permission of the Harry Ransom Humanities Research Center, University of Texas at Austin.

Preface

D. H. Lawrence's *Lady Chatterley's Lover* was first published in July 1928 in Florence, Italy. In 1959 Grove Press issued the first American unexpurgated edition of the novel in New York, and in 1960 Penguin Books printed the novel in England. In this study, I use the 1968 Bantam Books unexpurgated 1928 Orioli edition because it is still readily available in paperback and because it contains Lawrence's "A Propos of *Lady Chatterley's Lover,*" an essay that often helps us understand what Lawrence was trying to say in this famous novel.

Of course, what Lawrence was trying to say has been the subject of countless numbers of books and essays. One more book on this novel may seem redundant. The purpose of this volume, however, is to introduce the novel to the student, and yet I'd like to make sure throughout, as much as I can within the limitations of this format, that I do not kill off Lawrence's vision with too much interpretation. That would, to paraphrase D. H. Lawrence in his comments on Cézanne, roll the tombstone of conventional opinion over the life in this novel. Because Lawrence's fiction has the unique capacity to make us squirm, to upset us, to critique the world with energy and insight, criticism, especially academic criticism at times, often responds with techniques that make his books seem comfortable. If we listen to the critics instead of to the characters in his novels, we will find ourselves, as E. M. Forster says in *Aspects of the Novel,* moving round this book instead of through it.

Why should we listen to what Lawrence called the "low, calling cries" of his characters? Because, as he said, the novel is the "book of life."[1] Turn to the novel, he said, "and see wherein you are man alive, and wherein you are dead man in life . . . in the novel you can see, plainly, where the man goes dead, the woman goes inert. You can develop an instinct for life."[2] Finding out whether we have "instincts" for life is no picnic when we read a Lawrence book: it can be a painful experience. Yet it is this kind of reading experience that allows us to listen to the novel as it describes a struggle for love. Lawrence's own words are more appropriate here:

> An author should be in among the crowd, kicking their shins or cheering on to some mischief or merriment. . . . After all the world is *not* a stage—not to me: . . . nor a show-house of any sort. And art, especially novels, are not little theatres where the reader sits aloft and watches—like a god with a twenty-lira ticket—and sighs, commiserates, condones and smiles. That's what you want a book to be: because it leaves you so safe and so superior, with your two-dollar ticket to the show. And that's why my books are not and never will be . . . whoever reads me will be in the thick of the scrimmage, and if he doesn't like it—if he wants a safe seat in the audience—let him read somebody else.[3]

For their helpful suggestions and advice, I thank Robert Lecker, general editor of the Masterwork Series, Lewis DeSimone, former editor at Twayne Publishers, and India Koopman, editor. For his reading of this book in manuscript and for his helpful commentary, I thank Wayne Burns, a good teacher who over the years has deinstitutionalized Lawrence in his classroom. And for her unfailing ear for the false, I thank my wife, Patricia.

All references to the novel and to Lawrence's essay "A Propos of *Lady Chatterley's Lover*" are cited in the text (as *LCL* and "A Propos," respectively). Sections of this book first appeared in *Liberal and Fine Arts Review* 5, no. 1 (1985), and are reprinted by permission of the editors.

All quotations from D. H. Lawrence's poems are from *The Complete Poems of D. H. Lawrence* by D. H. Lawrence, Edited by V. de Sola Pinto & F. W. Roberts. Copyright © 1964, 1971 by Angelo Ravagli and C. M. Weekley, Executors of the Estate of Frieda Lawrence Ravagli. Used by permission of Viking Penguin, a division of Penguin Books USA Inc.

Chronology:
D. H. Lawrence's Life and Works

1885   David Herbert Lawrence born 11 September in Eastwood, Nottinghamshire, England, the fourth child of Arthur Lawrence, a coal miner who often spoke in dialect, and Lydia Beardsall, a former schoolteacher who spoke the King's English.

1898   Attends Nottingham High School on scholarship.

1901   Brother William (William in *Sons and Lovers*) dies. Meets frequently with Jessie Chambers (Miriam in *Sons and Lovers*) at Haggs Farm. Works in a surgical appliance factory, but leaves after first serious attack of pneumonia.

1902   Studies at the British School, Eastwood, as pupil-teacher.

1906   Begins two-year teacher-training at University College, Nottingham, after placing first on a scholarship examination.

1907   Writes first poems and short stories and begins first novel, *The White Peacock*. Wins *Nottinghamshire Guardian* short-story contest. Is acutely aware of the beauty and vibrancy of nature and of the ugliness of industrialization.

1908   Receives teaching certificate, accepts a position at a boy's school near London. Questions conventional religious faith.

1909   Early poems and stories are published in the *English Review*, edited by Ford Madox Ford. Meets London literary figures.

1910   Mother dies of cancer on 9 December. With Helen Corke, fellow schoolteacher, writes his second novel, *The Trespasser*. With Jessie Chambers, begins writing his first great novel, *Sons and Lovers*. Breaks with Jessie Chambers and becomes engaged to Louie Burrows, fellow student at college.

Chronology

1911   *The White Peacock* is published. "Odour of Chrysanthemums" is published in the *English Review*. Serious attack of pneumonia forces end to teaching.

1912   Resigns from teaching, breaks with Louie Burrows, and meets Frieda von Richthofen, wife of Professor Ernest Weekley, Lawrence's former language teacher, at University College, Nottingham. Leaves England with Frieda, travels to Germany, walks over the Tyrolese Alps, and settles in Gargnano, Italy, to finish *Sons and Lovers*. *The Trespasser* is published; starts *The Lost Girl* and a series of poems.

1913   *Love Poems and Others* published in February, *Sons and Lovers* in May. Begins writing what will become two novels, together considered his masterwork, *The Rainbow* and *Women in Love*. Works on travel book *Twilight in Italy*, poems, short stories, essays, and plays. Returns to England with Frieda and begins friendships with Edward Garnet, J. Middleton Murry, and Katherine Mansfield.

1914   Marries Frieda in London on 13 July. World War I begins. Short-story collection *The Prussian Officer* is published. Takes a walking tour of the Lake District, works on *Study of Thomas Hardy*, and argues in letters to friends and editors that he is doing something original in *The Rainbow*.

1915   Publishes *The Rainbow*, which is immediately suppressed by court order. Meets Aldous Huxley, Bertrand Russell, E. M. Forster, and Lady Ottoline Morrell (Hermione in *Women in Love*). Plans utopian art colony with friends. "England My England" published in *English Review*.

1916   Moves to Cornwall to finish *Women in Love*. *Twilight in Italy* and poetry collection *Amores* are published. Writes "The Horse Dealer's Daughter."

1917   Begins work on *Studies in Classic American Literature*. *Look! We Have Come Through* is published. Badgered by military authorities, medically examined, and found unfit for military service. He and Frieda, daughter of a German baron and cousin to the German flying ace Manfred von Richthofen, are expelled from Cornwall as "German spies." Begins work on *Aaron's Rod*.

1918   Writes *Movements in European History*, publishes *New Poems*, is reexamined by the army, and decides to leave England. Writes "The Fox," "The Blind Man," and "Tickets Please."

1919   Ill with influenza, Lawrence moves to Italy. Settles with Frieda in Capri. Publishes *Bay: A Book of Poems*.

Chronology

1920   *Women in Love* is published 9 November in New York. With Frieda in Capri, Florence, and Taormina, Sicily, Lawrence begins work on *Birds Beasts, and Flowers. The Lost Girl* published, wins James Tait Black prize. Works on *Psychoanalysis and the Unconscious* and *Mr. Noon.*

1921   Publishes *Sea and Sardina* as well as *Fantasia of the Unconscious* and short-story collection *England, My England.* Leaves for Australia, visits Ceylon. Writes *Kangaroo.* Leaves for Taos, New Mexico, where he will write, make furniture, and build a bread oven at a ranch.

1923   Visits Mexico City and Lake Chapala and begins *The Plumed Serpent.* Publishes *Studies in Classic American Literature, Kangaroo,* and *Birds, Beasts, and Flowers.* Writes *The Boy in the Bush* and "Surgery for the Novel—or a Bomb." Frieda returns to England.

1924   Returns to London, joins Frieda, and asks friends to begin a community at the ranch in Taos. Travels to France and Germany and returns to Taos, where he writes *St. Mawr,* "The Princess," "The Woman Who Rode Away," and parts of *Mornings in Mexico.* Travels to Oaxaca, Mexico, and rewrites *The Plumed Serpent. The Boy in the Bush* is published. Father, Arthur Lawrence, dies 10 September.

1925   Ill with malaria, Lawrence leaves Mexico for Taos. Finishes *The Plumed Serpent.* Writes plays, essays ("Why the Novel Matters"), reviews, and short stories. *St. Mawr* is published. Returns to England and then Italy. Writes "Sun." Diagnosed with tuberculosis.

1926   Moves with Frieda to the Villa Mirenda, near Florence. *The Plumed Serpent* is published. Makes his last visit to England and is moved by the effects of a coal strike. Visits his birthplace at Eastwood in July. By October back at Villa Mirenda, where he writes *The First Lady Chatterley* and begins to paint. Publishes "The Rocking Horse Winner."

1927   Tours the Etruscan tombs and begins *Etruscan Places.* Writes *The Escaped Cock. Mornings in Mexico* published. Second version of *Lady Chatterley (John Thomas and Lady Jane)* written and final draft begun.

1928   *Lady Chatterley's Lover* is published in July by arrangement with Giuseppe Orioli, a Florence bookseller. The novel will sell well, receive hostile reviews, and endure censorship well into the late 1950s. Lawrence moves to Switzerland, visits Germany, and writes "Introduction to These Paintings."

Postal authorities seize *Pansies*. *Collected Poems* and *The Woman Who Rode Away and Other Stories* published. Writes essays later to appear in *Phoenix*.

1929   Goes to Paris to discuss further editions of *Lady Chatterley*. Writes "A Propos of *Lady Chatterley's Lover*." Publishes *The Escaped Cock* and "Pornography and Obscenity." Paintings exhibited at the Warren Gallery in London are raided by the police. Treated in Bavaria for tuberculosis. Writes *Nettles, Last Poems,* and *Apocalypse*.

1930   Enters the Ad Astra sanitarium in Vence, southern France, on 6 February. Maria and Aldous Huxley help Lawrence move to a nearby villa 1 March. Lawrence dies of tuberculosis 2 March and is buried in Vence.

1935   Ashes taken to Taos, New Mexico, and placed there in a shrine above the ranch.

1944   Frieda authorizes the New York Dial Press edition of *The First Lady Chatterley*. Copies seized, but court declares the book not obscene.

1956   Frieda dies in Taos. Buried at the shrine.

1959   Grove Press in New York issues *Lady Chatterley's Lover* in the first American unexpurgated edition. Postmaster general finds the book obscene, but court hearing permits the novel to be carried in the U.S. mail.

1960   In England, Penguin Books successfully challenges British ban on *Lady Chatterley's Lover* by jury trial. For the first time the novel can be freely sold and read in England.

1972   All three versions of *Lady Chatterley* available.

LITERARY AND HISTORICAL CONTEXT

United States District Court

SOUTHERN DISTRICT OF NEW YORK

GROVE PRESS, INC. and READERS'
SUBSCRIPTION, INC.,

Plaintiffs,

— against —

ROBERT K. CHRISTENBERRY, individually and as Postmaster of the City of New York,

Defendant.

Civil 147–87
OPINION

BRYAN, *District Judge:*

These two actions against the Postmaster of New York, now con-
solidated, arise out of the denial of the United States mails to the recently published Grove Press unexpurgated edition of "Lady Chatterley's Lover" by D. H. Lawrence.

Plaintiffs seek to restrain the Postmaster from enforcing a decision
of the Post Office Department that the unexpurgated "Lady Chatterley's
Lover," and circulars announcing its availability, are non-mailable under
the statute barring obscene matter from the mails (18 U. S. C. § 1461).[1]
They also seek a declaratory judgment to the effect (1) that the novel is
not "obscene, lewd, lascivious, indecent or filthy" in content or character, and is not non-mailable under the statute or, in the alternative, (2)
that if the novel be held to fall within the purview of the statute, the
statute is to that extent invalid and violates plaintiffs' rights in contra-
vention of the First and Fifth Amendments.

Grove Press, Inc., one of the plaintiffs, is the publisher of the book.
Readers' Subscription, Inc., the other plaintiff, is a book club which has
rights to distribute it.

---

[1] The relevant portions of § 1461 provide:

"Every obscene, lewd, lascivious, indecent, filthy or vile article * * * and
"Every written or printed * * * circular, * * * or notice of any kind giving information * * * where, or how, or from whom * * * any of such
* * * articles * * * may be obtained * * *
"Is declared to be nonmailable matter and shall not be conveyed in the
mails or delivered from any post office or by any letter carrier."

The statute provides penalties for violation of up to five years imprisonment and
a maximum fine of $5,000 for a first offense and up to ten years' imprisonment and
a maximum $10,000 fine for subsequent offenses.

Court proceedings on the publication of *Lady Chatterley's Lover* in America.
Reprinted from D. H. Lawrence, *Sex, Literature, and Censorship,* ed. H. T.
Moore, Viking Press, 1953, p. 112.

1

From History to the "Country in Between"

Ours is essentially a tragic age, so we refuse to take it tragically.
—*Lady Chatterley's Lover*

Brief historical reviews in introductory literary textbooks often fix and label authors according to historical trends or classify novels according to critical tendencies. But for novelists—perhaps especially D. H. Lawrence—the "fact that their pens are in their hands is far more vivid to them" than their shifting sense of who or what they are according to academia.[1] The following review is not intended to cement *Lady Chatterley's Lover* onto a flat line in history in order to reduce its controversial content or tame the prophecy of its author; rather, my intention is to help make clear what Lawrence offered as a solution to the historical nightmare from which he sought to escape. Lawrence was no doubt influenced by the tumultuous events around him in the years between the two world wars; but as we read this novel, with a painful sense of how history affected the lives of its characters, we need to remind ourselves that it preserves Lawrence's fight for life in ways that make his struggle our aesthetic experience. In reading *Lady*

3

Chatterley's Lover, we find out if Lawrence's sense of history can change our sense of life.

By the time D. H. Lawrence was born in the mining village of Eastwood, Nottinghamshire, in 1885, England, still calling itself "the workshop of the world," was threatened by sharp agricultural declines and emerging industrial unrest. Class hatreds were growing, statistical research had affirmed the awful conditions of slum life in London and other large cities, and the famous English countrysides were scarred with industrial blight and ugliness. The agricultural England of the past had finally given way to the Industrial Revolution of the nineteenth century. By the 1900s, ironic contrasts were common: the Independent Labour party appeared in the English House of Commons, yet industrial strikes increased; tenuous political peace treaties eventually led to the Great War in 1914; postwar peace was marred by economic recessions and emerging political dictatorships; economic booms that brought wealth and material conveniences collapsed into the great market crash of October 1929.

Europe's postwar years of shaky recovery and retrenchment (1918–29) were felt most keenly in England and Germany. The Versailles Treaty with Germany had demanded reparations from the German government. Yet the English prime minister, Lloyd George, worked toward allowing flexible payments for the sake of economic recovery and cooperation, despite the fact that England had serious problems of its own. English wartime factories were closed, railways were returned to private ownership, and the plight of English coal miners remained England's most difficult problem during the 1920s. Coal miners wanted the government to keep their mines nationalized, but in 1921, because of coal export failures, the government divested itself of the industry. Unemployment rose sharply, wages were cut, and for the first time Lawrence saw the ravages of unrest in his native village. Lawrence's father, Arthur, had worked at the Brinsley Colliery, and the Lawrence family had known security and a rising standard of living. In fact, although Lawrence's essay "Nottingham and the Mining Countryside" (1929) gives a somewhat idyllic picture of working life in the mines, it is apparently not too far off the mark.[2] He called his birthplace the country of his heart.

In this queer jumble of the old England and the new, I came into
consciousness . . . life was a curious cross between industrialism
and the old agricultural England of Shakespeare and Milton and
Fielding and George Eliot. The dialect was broad Derbyshire, and
always "thee" and "thou." The people lived almost entirely by
instinct, men of my father's age could not really read. And the pit
did not mechanize men . . . the underground remoteness of the pit
"stall," and the continual presence of danger, made the physical,
instinctive, and intuitional contact between men very highly
developed, a contact almost as close as touch, very real and very
powerful . . . and if I think of my childhood, it is always as if there
was a lustrous sort of inner darkness, like the gloss of coal, in
which we moved and had our real being.[3]

By the time Lawrence decided to visit his home village of
Eastwood in 1926, before his death from tuberculosis in 1930, fear of
civil war between workers and employers contributed to the defeat
of the Labour party and fueled the general strike of 4 May 1926.
Winston Churchill had called the strikers dangerous to the state, and
Lawrence himself feared civil war. Probably more than at any other
time in his life, Lawrence felt deeply depressed about what had
become of the men and women who had lived and worked in his village. "The great crime which the moneyed classes and promoters of
industry committed in the palmy Victorian days was the condemning
of the workers to ugliness, ugliness, ugliness: meanness and formless
and ugly surroundings, ugly ideals, ugly religion, ugly hope, ugly love,
ugly clothes, ugly furniture, ugly houses, ugly relationship between
workers and employers" ("Nottingham," 138).

Underneath the visible chaos of British economics lurked subtle
but equally visible social changes. Skimpier clothing for women, jazz,
and birth control became popular in the 1920s. The first talking movies
came to London from Hollywood, and American "movie stars" became
popular in England. Increased sales of cars spawned a quicker pace of
life, and the cities and suburbs grew more crowded. Men and women
felt free to pursue the "good life," and the "bright young things," as
they were called, found themselves cited as examples of modern love
and mores. Lawrence would describe their sexual behavior in the open-

ing chapters of *Lady Chatterley's Lover,* as well as in essays with titles like "Making Love to Music" and "Sex versus Loveliness" or in his poems "Film Passion," "Image-Making Love," and "True Love at Last."

As he finished three full drafts of *Lady Chatterley,* Lawrence would feel, deeply, the tensions exhibited by English history from 1926 to 1930. Tensions between individual fulfillment and social manipulation, for example, one of the themes of the novel, find rich support in this history. In 1927, after Lawrence finished the first draft of the novel, which he wanted to call "Tenderness," there were social-ist riots in Vienna. In 1928, as Lawrence wrote the final draft of the novel, one that denies the possibility of politics as a solution to our personal problems, Mussolini published his *My Autobiography* and George Bernard Shaw his *Intelligent Woman's Guide to Socialism and Capitalism.* And after *Lady Chatterley's Lover* was finally published in Florence, it was attacked by the British press and banned by the police, while Hemingway's A *Farewell to Arms* and Remarque's *All Quiet on the Western Front* were hailed as masterpieces. Lawrence's paintings and poems were also seized by the police in 1928, and he wrote one of his famous essays in defense: "Pornography and Obscenity." Finally, in 1930, after Lawrence's death on 2 March, the Nazi party in Germany gained considerable ground in elections.[4]

Nevertheless, against this historical background, against the class divisions, urban squalor, and crazy politics, we see Lawrence fighting to become free from these tensions to get back *not* to what he called in "Return to Bestwood" the "Utopia of goodness" proposed by political leaders, the "upper" classes, but back to the searching of "one's own soul, for a way out into a new destiny . . . I know our vision of life is all wrong. We must be prepared to have a new conception of what it means, *to live,*" to be "sensitive to life and to its movements."[5] And by "to live" Lawrence means struggling to remain individuals in our sen-sitivity to life, the way the characters Connie and Mellors in *Lady Chatterley's Lover* struggle to retain a bit of their individuality in spite of a modern, mechanized, historical world.

Like the boy growing up on a California beach near the nuclear plant at San Onofre, with its noiseless smashing of atoms, or like the boy on the dunes of Lake Michigan who swims and frolics near U.S.

Steel, with its thunderous toil inside and its massive lay-offs, so Lawrence grew up amidst the contrasts in the Erewash Valley district of England, with its old forests and new coal mines. The colliers, Lawrence said, "have an underneath ache and heaviness very much like my own. . . . They are the only people who move me strongly, and with whom I feel myself connected in deeper destiny. . . . I shrink away from them, and I have an acute nostalgia for them" ("Bestwood," 264–65). This shrinking away and attraction, Lawrence's intense ambivalence, is our ambivalence to the modern world. The tension it gives us, as it gave Lawrence and his characters in *Lady Chatterley's Lover,* is an "ache and heaviness," a kind of muffled weight in our hearts as we walk into a forest.

"There was a sense of latent wildness and unbrokenness," said Lawrence, "a weird sense of thrill and adventure in the pitch-dark Midland nights. . . . The *country in between* the colliery regions had a lonely sort of fierceness and beauty."[6] *Lady Chatterley's Lover* describes this important *country in between* the mines and the cities, as well as that tense serenity of our psychic landscape underneath history. "If England is to be regenerated," said Lawrence in "A Propos of *Lady Chatterley's Lover,*" "then it will be by the arising of a new blood-contact" between men and women, and between men and women and nature" ("A Propos," 352).

> When the vast, vast masses of men have been caught by the
>   machine
> into the industrial dance of the living death,
> . . . .
> Then must a single man die with them, in the clutch of
>   iron?
> Or must he try to amputate himself from the iron-
>   entangled body of mankind
> and risk bleeding to death, but perhaps escape into some
>   unpopular place.[7]

Lady Chatterley's Lover is a novel whose response to history was and still is unpopular indeed, as we shall see in the next chapter.

2

"To Smash Up the Vast Lie of the World"

Lawrence himself, is, as far as I know, the only prophetic novelist writing today.

—E. M. Forster, *Aspects of the Novel*

If you're a novelist, you know that paradise is in the palm of your hand, and on the end of your nose, because both are alive; and alive, and man alive, which is more than you can say, for certain, of paradise. . . . And being a novelist, I consider myself superior to the saint, the scientist, the philosopher and the poet . . . at its best the novel . . . can help you . . . not to be a dead man in life.

—D. H. Lawrence, "Why the Novel Matters"

Even before the publication of *Lady Chatterley's Lover* in 1928, Lawrence knew that he had written something no one before had dared to write. "I am in a quandary about my novel," he said in a letter. "It's what the world would call very improper. But you know it's not really improper—I always labor at the same thing, to make the sex relation valid and precious, instead of shameful. And this novel is the furthest I've gone. To me it is beautiful and tender and frail as the naked self is, and I shrink very much even from having it typed" (*Collected Letters,* 2:972). With *Lady Chatterley's Lover,* Lawrence wanted to make a clear and powerful *"adjustment in consciousness to the basic physical realities"* (*Collected Letters,* 2:1111), as he put it, and to describe, openly and honestly, the life-giving powers of sex. At its publication the world, of course, did condemn it, and Scotland Yard did seize it. Yet we still read it, study it, and argue about it. Why?

First of all, *Lady Chatterley's Lover* is indeed the first serious novel in English literature to give us candid and honest descriptions of sexual intercourse. But Lawrence did not set out to do this to change the direction of English literature, nor was he interested in shocking or titillating us to promote "liberation." And if we take him at his word in his essays and letters, neither was he advocating a return to primitive living or calling for people to go out looking for their Connie or for their Mellors.[1] (Diana Trilling writes in "Letter to a Young Critic" that when she and her friends first read Lawrence, they thought "his metaphors were translatable into a program for practical conduct!"[2]) It was not Lawrence's intention to give us codes for conduct or a new sex-idealism. Rather, the novel shows how we "have to go back, a long way, before the idealist conceptions begin, before Plato, before the tragic idea of life arose, to get on to our feet again. For the gospel of salvation through the Ideals and escape from the body coincided with the tragic conception of human life" ("A Propos," 354–55). This is the important point Lawrence illustrates in the plot and theme of *Lady Chatterley's Lover,* and it is the dramatization of this point that allows the novel to remain something we want to keep reading.

Yet we keep reading this novel for other reasons, too, for the book proposes that both our ruining of the earth's natural beauty and our mad pursuit of money are really the results of our lack of sexual fulfillment. Denying the importance of our bodies, Lawrence says, leads to the kind of destruction of nature that is anchored in our jealousy of her beauty and to the frenetic pursuit of money and success that is nothing but a substitute for sexual peace. It is difficult to describe these ideas as "themes" in the novel, however, since Lawrence's ideas are more like messages, signals sent back to us from someone on a distant search for meaning, like telegraphic communications from a dark outpost. Here are some of the communiqués, as it were, that ensure the importance of this novel.

ON THE NATURAL WORLD

Lawrence believed nature to be regenerative for human beings, and the relationship between Connie and Mellors and the woods in *Lady Chatterley's Lover* is just that. In chapter 12, for example, as Connie goes into the woods to meet Mellors and walks by primroses that are "full of pale abandon" and "no longer shy," she, too, seems to be full of abandon and no longer shy. The woods help her feel more alive. Lawrence carefully uses natural imagery to show how new growth in nature parallels the new emotional growth in Connie. All living things, for Lawrence, are in active relation with one another, whether they know it or not, and when that living relation is severed, then Lawrence says men fail to live.

In chapter 10, Connie is described as having in her a tenderness like that of growing hyacinths, and the trees in the woods near Wragby Hall, where Mellors lives, glisten "naked and dark as if they had unclothed themselves" (*LCL*, 130), as Connie and Mellors will, after walking through a wall of "prickly trees," unclothe themselves. In Lawrence's natural world the basic elements of nature—fire, rock, water, and earth—and the basic elements of men and women—their male and female *plasm*—are equally important, equally natural. "We need to put off our personality," Lawrence said, "even our individuality, and enter the region of the elements. . . . The primary human psyche is a complex plasm, which quivers, sense-conscious, in contact with the circumambient cosmos."[3] When plasm begins to live in us, it becomes dangerous, challenging our complacency about the way we live. For Lawrence, the awareness and experience of natural plasm can provide the needed physical counterweight to our lopsidedly mental lives.

On Men, Women, and Love

Lawrence's powerful message about love is given full expression in *Lady Chatterley's Lover*. In it we learn right away that for Lawrence love is not something nice, pretty, or idealistic; love is not a goal or an ideal but a force of disruption and creation. What love creates is the "separate clarity of being, unthinkable otherness and separateness."[4] Two people in love connect, but they remain isolated like "gems," and in the passion of sensuality they are "burned into essentiality," jolted into the essential male and female. Love is fusion and separateness, and in this duality, Lawrence says, there is fulfillment ("Love," 154).

There is "no getting away from the fact that the blood of woman is dynamically polarized in opposition, or in difference to the blood of man," Lawrence writes, "yet the great outstanding fact of the individuality even of the blood makes us need a corresponding individuality in the woman we are to embrace."[5] This is a good description of the love between Connie and Mellors in chapters 10 through 12. When Lawrence uses the phrase "polarized in opposition" he does not mean that men and women do not need one another—for they do, he says, in order to be whole. The sexes are not by nature pitted against each other in hostility. It happens, in Lawrence's view, only in certain periods: when man loses unconscious faith in himself, and woman loses her faith in him, unconsciously and then consciously. It is not a biological sex struggle. Not at all. "Sex is the great uniter, the great unifier. Only in periods of the collapse of instinctive life-assurance in men does sex become a great weapon and divider."[6] Connie had "connected" Mellors "up again," Lawrence tells us in chapter 10, "when he wanted to be alone. She had cost him that bitter privacy of a man who at last wants only to be alone" (*LCL*, 125).

On Money

In a poem entitled "Money-Madness," Lawrence says that we grovel before money in "strange terror" because it is our "vast collective madness" (*Complete Poems,* 486). And in our groveling we fear our "money-mad fellow-men" because we hear them say: "How much is he worth? / Has he no money? Then let him eat dirt, and go cold" (486). Lawrence doesn't hate money, but he does say that we are obsessed by it. We pursue it to fill a void left by the modern "collapse of instinctive life-assurance" ("The Real Thing," 197).

Nowhere does Lawrence describe this collapse more vividly than in chapter 11 of *Lady Chatterley's Lover.* "England, my England! But which is *my* England?" the chapter asks. The England of old, with its agriculture and old halls, or the new, with its brittle little mining villages, its big cities and pursuits? "The younger generation were utterly unconscious of the old England. There was a gap in the continuity of consciousness, almost American: but industrial really" (*LCL,* 170). As Connie takes her car trip through Tevershall in this chapter, we are presented with descriptions of the collapse.

> The car ploughed uphill through the long squalid straggle of Tevershall, the blackened brick dwellings, the black slate roofs glistening their sharp edges, the mud black with coal-dust, the pavements wet and black. It was as if dismalness had soaked through and through everything. The utter negation of natural beauty, the utter negation of the gladness of life, the utter absence of the instinct for shapely beauty which every bird and beast has, the utter death of the human intuitive faculty was appalling . . . the England of today . . . was producing a new race of mankind, over-conscious in the money and social and political side, on the spontaneous, intuitive side dead,—but dead. (162–64)

In his letter to Connie at the end of the novel, Mellors complains that "The young ones get mad because they've no money to spend . . . [if] you could only tell them that living and spending isn't the same thing!" (325–26). Lawrence's analysis of our money madness, our success mongering, is very precise: the pursuit of money and the pursuit of acquisitive love are twin symptoms of what he calls the cancer of our civilization—acquisitiveness, the constant feeling of power we get through the endless acquiring of things and people.

Connie Chatterley is fleeing from all this, and that's why in chapter 12, in a scene to counter the Tevershall sequence, Connie goes "directly" into the woods, where primroses are "broad, and full of pale abandon," where "columbines were unfolding their ink-purple riches," where everywhere there were "bud-knots and the leap of life!" (*LCL*, 177). In the love scene that follows, the acquisitive ego in both Connie and Mellors is put to rest and the language Mellors uses to describe Connie's body is seen by us as regenerative as the nature that surrounds the couple.

On Language

Lady Chatterley's Lover is really the first book in English to get us to at least "think sexually, complete, and clear," even if we can't "act sexually to our complete satisfaction" ("A Propos," 332). Since the novel does not present sex-language as the "dirty little secret" we can thrill to, the way we thrill to it in some movies, music, T.V., and popular fictions, the book is still, today, misunderstood. Sex-excitement of the secretive sort, what Lawrence calls in his famous essay "Pornography and Obscenity" a "mob-habit," is very different from the "plain and simple excitement, quite open and wholesome, which you find in some Boccaccio stories [and should not be] for a minute . . . confused with the furtive excitement aroused by rubbing the dirty little secret in all secrecy in modern bestsellers."[7]

Underneath our mob-reaction to sex, our intellectual anger at having language arouse feelings in us, is another awareness, one that, if we are honest, fills us with neither indignation nor condemnation. It is an awareness that we get when we listen to the "voices of the honourable beasts that call in the dark paths of the veins of our body. . . . Listening inwards, inwards, not for words nor for inspiration, but to the lowing of the innermost beasts, the feelings" ("Feelings," 759). And when we do listen to our feelings, we realize that they live in our solitary self, with its careful offerings and requests—its *senses' tender*. Can we listen to our feelings? Lawrence answers that if we can't, then we can at least "look in the real novels, and there listen-in" to the "low, calling cries of the characters" ("Feelings," 760). These "low, calling cries of the characters" in *Lady Chatterley's Lover* are the sometimes reluctant but desirous and tender offerings of love between Connie and Mellors, their *senses' tender* as they are described by Lawrence's special language. If, then, we are honest, what we really feel indignant about is how pornography attempts to "insult sex, to do dirt on it," to make sex a secret, never "fully and openly conscious" ("Pornography," 181). *Lady Chatterley's Lover* is Lawrence's attempt to smash the secret, to destroy pornography, to have fictional characters at least "think sexually, complete, and clear." This is the reason why the novel is so important and why so many authors since have tried (and failed) to write novels similar to it.[8]

But isn't *Lady Chatterley's Lover* still pornography, in the sense that we can't help *thinking* about what the author describes? Doesn't Lawrence's creative language trap us into making circular arguments about this novel? We might say to ourselves: "Thinking clearly about the sex scenes is still thinking about sex, but doesn't Lawrence want me to stop getting sex into my head?" Sigmund Freud said that the language of a novel is a kind of "fore-pleasure," allowing the release of "tensions in our minds" through identification with the characters in order to "enjoy our own day-dreams without self-reproach or shame."[9] Difficult as it was, Lawrence tried to write a novel that would avoid this mental foreplay. How did he try to do this? First, he steadfastly refused to describe the struggle for love between Connie and Mellors in sentimental terms. Sentimentality, he said, is always the first sign of pornography, because all it does is tickle the old secret about sex ("Pornography," 185). Second, in a remark that he made to his wife, Frieda, after finishing the first draft of the novel, we hear a resolve on his part to fight the mental foreplay that fiction can produce: "The tenderness and gentleness [in the novel] hadn't enough punch and fight in it, it was a bit wistful."[10] This "punch and fight" against being wistful is the fight against the "sentimental lie of purity," Lawrence writes. Inside himself or in the outside world "a man must come to the limits of himself and become aware of something beyond him . . . [what] surpasses me is the very urge of life that is within me, and this life urges me to forget myself and to yield to the stirring half-born impulse to smash up the vast lie of the world, and make a new world" ("Pornography," 185). As we shall see, *Lady Chatterley's Lover* describes this "urge of life" and shows us how Connie and Mellors fight the "vast lie of the world." Moreover, it is our experience of their fight that prevents us from turning the novel into mob-porn or from reading the book in a way that reinforces mental foreplay. The importance of *Lady Chatterley's Lover* rests on this crucial point. For it is the fight or struggle for love that helps us not to be a "dead man in life," as Lawrence said in "Why the Novel Matters." "No other writer," says Wayne Burns, "has ever attempted to reproduce feelings such as this in anything like such detail . . . the zig-zag, the see-saw, the dialectic of the man-woman relationship." This, he says, is "Lawrence's greatest contribution to fiction and to art in general."[11]

3

Rolling Back the Stone

The novel has a future. It's got to have the courage to tackle new propositions without using abstractions; it's got to present us with new, really new feelings . . . it's got to break a way through, like a hole in the wall. And the public will scream and say it is a sacrilege.
—D. H. Lawrence, "Surgery for the Novel—Or a Bomb"

After Lawrence published *Lady Chatterley's Lover* in Florence, Italy, in July 1928, the outcry was heard all over England. This came as no surprise to Lawrence, since his typist and other friends had reacted badly to early drafts of the novel. The initial fuss over the book, and the reason it was banned until 1960, centered, of course, on the explicit sexual language. With the exception of his wife, Frieda, a few friends like Maria and Aldous Huxley, and various sympathetic publishers in France and Italy, critics and "practically all" his friends, Lawrence said, turned his "real emotions" in this novel to ridicule ("A Propos," 337). Reactions in the British press were strong: the 14 October 1928 *Sunday Chronicle* labeled the novel as "reeking with obscenity" and reported that British customs authorities had seized the book. On 20 October the popular magazine *John Bull* called the novel a "landmark" in evil, created "out of the turgid vigour of a poisoned genius."[1] John Middleton Murray, formerly a close friend of Lawrence, did say the novel was important and valuable, but his review attacked his former friend (Draper, 281–84). Writing for the *New Republic*, Edmund Wilson is really the only critic who fully understood the importance of *Lady Chatterley's Lover* during the 1920s. In dealing with sexual scenes, Wilson said, Lawrence "has greatly benefited by being able . . . to do without symbols and circumlocutions . . . it keeps these scenes recognizably human."[2]

In the late 1930s, English novelists Aldous Huxley, E. M. Forster, and Arnold Bennett did their best to describe Lawrence as one of our best modern writers, but they were alone in holding such a view. Noting Lawrence's explicit language, V. S. Pritchett said that Lawrence, in "straining after the sublime . . . overstrained and dropped into the ridiculous," and André Malraux claimed that Lawrence's eroticism was not the expression of individuals but a "state of life, in the same way that opium became part of the life of the Chinese" (Draper, 298, 294). James Joyce called the novel "Lady Chatterbox's Lover" and briefly implied that it was nothing more than a cheap piece of French pornography.[3] T. S. Eliot flatly called Lawrence "sick" for writing the book and claimed that, as readers, we too are "sick" for liking it.[4] Perhaps only Frieda Lawrence and W. B. Yeats understood what Lawrence was trying to do: "I wondered at his courage and daring to face these hidden things that people dare not write or say," said Frieda in her memoir, *"Not I, But the Wind . . ."*[5]; and Yeats described the novel this way: "Those two lovers, the gamekeeper and his employer's wife, each separated from their class by their love, and by fate, are poignant in their loneliness, and the course language of the one, accepted by both, becomes a forlorn poetry uniting their solitudes, something ancient, humble and terrible" (Draper, 298).

In 1944, the Dial Press in New York printed *The First Lady Chatterley,* initiating an attempt by authorities to ban the book. But after a New York court declared the novel was not obscene, the book received wide attention from national newspapers. Scant attention, however, was paid to the novel by critics in the 1940s. Only authors like W. H. Auden and Henry Miller were reading and commenting on it in print. Miller devoted a whole chapter to the novel in his *Sunday after the War* (1944), saying that in Mellors, Lawrence has stripped away from the male the ideal of the lover or husband. W. H. Auden, however, remarked that *Lady Chatterley's Lover* is "as pornographic as *Fanny Hill*" (Andrews, 50).

By the late 1950s most of the commentary on the novel dismissed it as illogical, in bad taste, or quasi-religious. In his *D. H. Lawrence: Portrait of a Genius But . . .* (1950), Richard Aldington mentions *Lady Chatterley's Lover* only in passing, saying that because Lawrence found a way out of the ugliness and heaviness of his native land through his love for his wife, Frieda, he then "leaped to the conclusion that salvation was to be achieved" for all of us "through 'phallic tenderness.' "[6] Mark Spilka's *The Love Ethic of D. H. Lawrence* (1955) called *Lady Chatterley's Lover* a novel "that projects no social program" but rather insists on a "change in the mode, condition, or quality" of our individual lives.[7] Spilka's further claim, however, that sex in the novel is a kind of "religious" experience, is not supported with references to the text.

Most surprising of all is the work of F. R. Leavis, often called the most important critic of Lawrence. His *D. H. Lawrence: Novelist* (1955) was the first full-fledged defense of Lawrence in England, and even as late as 1988 it was characterized as "the most influential book on Lawrence"[8] Oddly enough, however, Leavis does not discuss *Lady Chatterley's Lover* at length, and in fact even objects to it. The "willed insistence on the words and the facts [Lawrence's frank description of sexual intercourse] it seems to me, whatever the intention, [has] something unacceptable, something offensive about it," Leavis said.[9] He clearly states what he thinks that that *something* is: the book is an offense "against taste" (369). To save Lawrence for *taste*, Leavis puts him in what he calls the "great tradition" of the English novel.

Of course, Lawrence is not interested in appealing to our "good taste" (i.e., our safe feelings), as he makes clear in "A Propos." In fact, as he said in a letter to a friend while writing *Lady Chatterley's Lover:* "I feel one still has to fight for the phallic reality, as against the non-phallic cerebration unrealities."[10] No real fight is ever in good taste, and that's why the novel, in giving the reader a fight for his emotional and intellectual life, keeps knocking the wind out of the kind of criticism that wants Lawrence to be respectable. Lawrence said of the efforts to tame his book: "why should the red flower have its pistil nipped out?" (*Letters*, 6:322). Nevertheless, the efforts of 1950s critics to snip out the pistil from *Lady Chatterley's Lover* set the stage for similar cuttings in the 1960s–80s. These were the decades concerned with the nonphallic, cerebral unrealities of "form" (the structure of the novel), "myth" (labeling the book an Adam and Eve story), and "utopia" (pigeonholing the book as a failed attempt to provide a utopian solution to the industrial age).

Most critical commentary on the novel in the 1960s, still a little reluctant about discussing the sexual activity, relies heavily on biographical, symbolic, and sometimes psychoanalytical speculations to explain theme. Keith Sagar in *The Art of D. H. Lawrence* (1966) claims that Lawrence fuses the Christian myth of prelapsarian innocence (before the "Fall of Man") with a pagan phallicism in the scenes between Connie and Mellors. But copulation, he says, "looms out of all proportion to other activities in a fully human relationship." Sagar further maintains that the "symbolism of the phallus is hardly realised in the novel."[11] But Lawrence never intended his two main characters to be sexy Christians or innocent primitives, nor can the phallus in the book be a symbol for anything other than itself. Mellors's penis is just that, the way Hardy's pig pizzle is just what it is when Arabella throws it in Jude's face. Sagar's statement that you "cannot have a real man and a real woman in a real wood copulating with symbolic genitals" is, therefore, unintentionally humorous and ironic (197).

H. M. Daleski's *The Forked Flame* (1965) is the least squeamish study in its discussion of sex, but he laments that Lawrence does not convince us that Mellors can be sensual and tender with Connie, given the conditions of their famous last night of passion. Daleski concludes that the sensuality in this famous scene represents the return of male domination in Mellors and in Lawrence, thereby negating what the novel had been trying to establish—tenderness between the sexes.[12]

Wayne Burns takes issue with these kinds of comments by advising students and teachers alike to read what Lawrence had to say about his novel in "A Propos." He agrees that "Mellors is, in short,

Lawrence's idealized self-image. And that is why he is not always convincing as a character." "Yet if Mellors's preaching is obtrusive," Burns continues, "it enables Lawrence to present the full implications of the conflict between Connie . . . and Clifford—to show that Connie's struggle against Clifford is not merely a struggle for her own personal survival but the struggle of the human being against the deadly machinery of modern society."[13] Once, during a lecture, when Burns was asked why he had "chosen to talk about *Lady Chatterley* when there were all those other novels—*Sons and Lovers, The Rainbow, Women in Love*—novels filled with beautiful symbols," he replied that Lawrence had written *Lady Chatterley's Lover* to put an end to symbolic readings. "What Lawrence thought of this type of critical humbuggery—the type that would turn phalluses into symbols—he made clear time and again—most devastatingly, perhaps, in characterizing Cézanne's critics as "the good bourgeois corpses in their cultured winding sheets . . . [who] abstracted his good apple into Significant Form."[14] When critics mythicize and symbolize Lawrence, he continued, they "emasculate him and bring him into line with the ideas and ideals of our culture" (Burns 1968, 198). Kingsley Widmer's equally biting 1966 essay, "Notes on the Literary Institutionalization of D. H. Lawrence," rings true today. He calls most critical studies of the author simple adaptations of Lawrence to "established orders and repressive sensibilities."[15]

Commentary in the 1970s and 1980s continued the adaptation of *Lady Chatterley's Lover* to now familiar trends in academic criticism. We see no outright censoring, but we do see put to efficient use the ideological lenses of feminism, Marxism, mysticism, and structuralism. In fact, D. and F. B. Jackson admit that "many critics ignored the novel's treatment of sex altogether . . . preferring instead to discuss the book as a version of the utopian, as pastoral, or as a retelling of myth or medieval romance."[16] Ideological politics has played a significant role in the interpretation of the novel as well. Michael Squires—perhaps taking his cue from Scott Sanders's quasi-Marxist *D. H. Lawrence: The World of the Five Major Novels* (1973), which says that Lawrence was "driven again and again to flee history into a mythical realm in which the passions of the body redeem the cruelties of the world[17]—concludes in *The*

Creation of Lady Chatterley's Lover (1983) that "the ending might have been enhanced if Connie and Mellors had committed themselves to some politically useful work. In that way they would have demonstrated a connection, now lacking, between the politics of sex and the politics of class."[18] Peter Scheckner ends his *Class, Politics, and the Individual* (1985) with a similar lament: that since Lawrence stepped back from political radicalism, "the 'little forked flame' between the lovers is just that—little, barely warming anyone.[19]

There is also a curious anger at Lawrence the man, easily detected underneath the criticism of the 1970s and 1980s. On 3 February 1970, the Copley News Service released a story printed in newspapers across the United States with the title *"Lady Chatterley's Lover* Author Never Forgiven in Home Town." The article attacked Lawrence personally. In *Sexual Politics,* published a year later, Kate Millet called *Lady Chatterley's Lover* Lawrence's ugly prayer to the dominant male, and in *D. H. Lawrence and the Idea of the Novel* (1979) John Worthen said that Lawrence did not even know what he wanted a novel to be, that in his final isolation as a banned author he no longer even had a sense of his audience. Norman Mailer argued in his 1971 *The Prisoner of Sex* that Lawrence had the soul of a "passionate woman" that wanted to be a man, while others claimed Lawrence had homosexual leanings in his psychic makeup. Mark Spilka claimed Lawrence could finally, if not in life, at least "imagine the purging of his own self-importance and self-will" in the character of Mellors.[20]

Criticism in the late 1980s was characterized by a pronounced tendency to believe that the "last word" could be uttered about the novel. Keith Sagar's *D. H. Lawrence: Life into Art* (1985) gives *Lady Chatterley's Lover* only a page or two, accusing the novel of not living up to its "tragic possibilities." L. L. Martz states with last-word finality that *Lady Chatterley's Lover* is simply a "series of symbolic events, with commentary."[21] Most peculiar is Anthony Burgess's *Flame into Being* (1985), a book he calls his "tribute" to Lawrence. Speaking as a British novelist, and "paying a debt" to Lawrence for "enriching our lives" as the "pioneer of sexual frankness," Burgess goes on to characterize Lawrence's language in *Lady Chatterley's Lover* as "an aesthetic . . . gaffe," a mistake. He objects to Lawrence's use of the word "fuck" by saying it cannot imply love: "To talk of a fuck is to talk of a rapid release analogous to defecation."[22] Similar to defecation? Surely Burgess remembers Lawrence's discussion in "Pornography and Obscenity" of those people who equate the "sex flow" with the "excremental flow" ("Pornography," 176).

Has our current criticism returned, therefore, to the earlier condemnations of *Lady Chatterley's Lover* in the 1920s by omitting discussions of the novel in anthologies and critical studies, or by objecting, once again, to the language of the book? Perhaps. It is difficult to tell. Beneath all the glitzy and avant-garde criticism of our day, there still seems to be a clear tendency to condemn this novel, to corral it, to close it up once and for all and make it safe for democracy, to institutionalize it and thereby tame its liveliness, its natural bitterness, belligerence, and beauty. In their 1988 *Critical Essays on D. H. Lawrence* editors D. and F. B. Jackson complain that it is too "romantic" to point out the institutionalization of Lawrence, since he has provoked over 6,000 books and articles on his works. They claim it is useless to "complain that Lawrence's power to disturb is suffering entombment" (42–43). Nevertheless, at the risk of sounding "romantic," I believe Lawrence has, and continues to be, entombed. Time and again Lawrence described this process, especially in his remarks on how critics reacted to Cézanne: "Cézanne's apple hurts. It made people shout with pain. And it was not till his followers had turned him again into an abstraction that he was ever accepted. Then the critics stepped forth and abstracted his good apple into Significant Form, and henceforth Cézanne was saved. Saved for democracy. Put safely in the tomb again, and the stone rolled back."[23]

What Lawrence says happened to Cézanne's apple has happened to *Lady Chatterley's Lover.* The issue is not whether Lawrence's novel will continue to "inspire" criticism but whether criticism will continue to impose its ideologies on his novel and to bury it beneath mountains of commentary. This, Lawrence said in a letter to Carlo Linati, he would not abide: "You need not complain that I don't subject the intensity of my vision—or whatever it is—to some vast and imposing rhythm—by which you mean, isolate it on a stage, so that you can look down on it like a god who has got a ticket to the show. I never will . . ." (22 January 1925, *Collected Letters,* 2:827).

In the same letter Lawrence wrote that a "book should be either a bandit or a rebel or a man in a crowd. People should either run for their lives, or come under the colours, or say *how do you do?*" As a novel, *Lady Chatterley's Lover* is very much a bandit, a rebel, and *in the classroom* it remains alive, nimble, quite capable of throwing off the winding sheets of idealistic criticism, rolling back the stone, and walking out of the tomb. For the student, then, this novel keeps its power to corrode, undermine, fight, tackle new feelings, and break a hole in the culture wall.

A READING

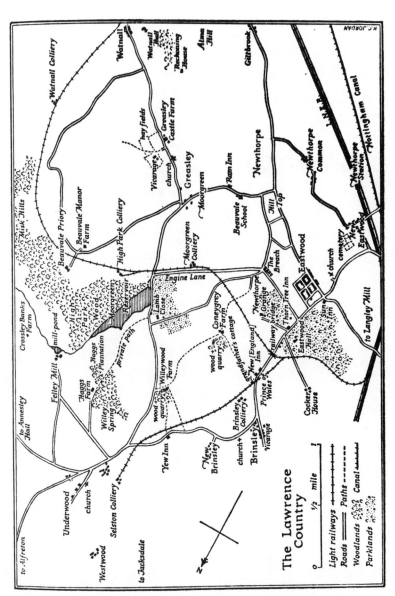

The Lawrence Country. Permission granted by Barnes & Noble Books, Totowa, New Jersey, and Macmillan.

4

Loss

Pull down my native village to the last brick. Plan a nucleus. Fix the focus.

—D. H. Lawrence, "Nottingham and the Mining Countryside"

"Why don't men and women really like one another nowadays?" Connie asked Tommy Dukes.

—*Lady Chatterley's Lover*

THE FIG LEAF

Getting kicked out of a sexual paradise is really nothing new. Powerful feelings often elicit equally powerful condemnations. Adam and Eve were the first to feel such condemnations from a jealous Being, so the story goes, and to finalize and make official their expulsion; we would later be shielded from sexual truths even in paintings of the famous pair. It was recently discovered, for example, that seventeenth-century artists painted fig leaves on Adam and Eve in Masaccio's c. 1425 fresco "The Expulsion from the Garden" in the Church of Santa Maria del Carmine in Florence, Italy. It is not surprising, then, that *Lady Chatterley's Lover,* published in Florence in 1928, should get its fig leaf too in order to censor the words and activities of an equally famous pair: Connie Chatterley and Oliver Mellors.

D. H. Lawrence's artistic intention in this novel was not to condemn his famous pair for their strong feelings but to support them and to describe their struggle for love completely, clearly, richly. But to do so he had to wrestle with what he saw English had become: a language stripped of real life and freedom by modern mores and warfare. In chapter 6, Connie thinks: "All the great words . . . were cancelled for her generation: love, joy, happiness, home, mother, father, husband, all these great, dynamic words were half dead now, and dying from day to day. . . . As for sex, the last of the great words, it was just a cocktail term for an excitement that bucked you up for a while, then left you more raggy than ever. Frayed! It was as if the very material you were made of was cheap stuff, and was fraying out to nothing" (*LCL,* 63–64).

In the first seven chapters of the novel—which are the focus of this chapter—the talk at Wragby Hall between Clifford Chatterley and his friends centers around these "cancelled" words and ideas. When they discuss what these words mean, especially the word *sex,* they feel, as human beings, that they are lost, lost in a world where these words have been stripped of their meaning, and so they give up, give up hoping for anything else. Connie, too, felt that resignation was the "simplest solution of the otherwise insoluble. She wanted nothing more than what she'd got; only she wanted to get ahead with what she'd got: Clifford, the stories, Wragby, the Lady-Chatterley business, money, and fame, such as it was . . . she wanted to go ahead with it all. Love, sex, all that sort of stuff, just water-ices! Lick it up and forget it. If you don't hang on to it in your mind, it's nothing. Sex especially . . . nothing!" (*LCL,* 65).

From the very first chapter, Lawrence makes it clear that *talking* is the important thing for the men and women of the modern world. "The arguments, the discussions were the great thing: the love-making and connection were only a sort of primitive reversion and a bit of an anticlimax" for Connie and her sister, Hilda (*LCL,* 3) (as well as for their boyfriends, really. For even the boys in Dresden loved with the "passion of mental attraction" [*LCL,* 5]). From beginning to end in this novel, there is tension between a dead talk that uses words people seem to have given up on, and alive, intimate sex. In all the important scenes, especially in those scenes between Connie and Mellors, Lawrence reinforces the idea that new feelings must find a language that fights against the deadliness of modern, mental life. Words like *glory* and *honor* had been stripped of their meaning by the insanity of trench warfare during World War I, and the word *love* had lost its mysterious, subversive, and regenerative meaning by being embalmed through countless repetitions in popular songs, product advertisements, and modern spite. "The tie that binds *us* just now," says Tommy Dukes, talking about modern life, "is mental friction on one another . . . the mental life seems to flourish with its roots in spite . . . [the] sheer spite of it all, just sheer joy in pulling somebody else to bits" (*LCL,* 36). Later in the novel, words like *glory, honor, courage, sex, love,* and *joy* will gain new meaning as we see the relationship between Connie and Mellors grow and fight against the world that surrounds them. These words will characterize the way Connie and Mellors preserve their independence, their integrity and sexual experiences, and will no longer be understood as words whose definitions are yoked to repressive social expectations.

For quite some time, people objected strongly to Lawrence's language in this novel, calling it vulgar, comical, or symbolic.[1] Nowadays, objections by scholars to Lawrence's words are fairly sophisticated. Some critics say Lawrence's attempt to use "four-letter" words was doomed from the beginning, because no matter how we may use them to talk about love, their connotations are too powerful, too mired in their social connotations. One critic stated that such words will or will not have their effect depending on one's personal background, and that for him "most of their magic had been rubbed off before he was out of grammar school."[2] But such critiques, dependent as they are on the assumption that schoolboy pruriency is the only response to Lawrence's explicit language, misread Lawrence's wider plan in the whole novel. For what Lawrence hopes for is our acceptance of those physical facts that the words denote. He wants to revitalize these words, dead and buried in social dirt as they are, by digging them out of our normal conversations, brushing the dirt off them, and putting them into the context of the whole novel as we read it, putting them into really new scenes, into new feelings. Context determines our reactions to these words, and, as we shall see, Lawrence's powerful sexual scenes are up to the task of changing our habitual reactions to the so-called "four-letter" words. Lawrence uses these words seriously in ways that "support neither an abusive nor a shameful nor a scornful connotation," as H. M. Daleski says in *The Forked Flame*. And, he continues, this is very different from the way James Joyce uses such words in *Ulysses;* for Joyce's use of them "perpetuates their debasement" (264). Other critics claim that Lawrence's language is inadequate because it cannot truly synthesize human sexual experience. (What language could?) But as Lydia Blanchard points out, "to see that Lawrence is both creating a language of the feelings and simultaneously calling into question the adequacy of that language is to see the very brilliance of the novel."[3]

And finally, one critic says that since Mellors's phallic language is "hard to reconcile with the holy rites of intercourse." Lawrence engaged in a "misguided foray into phallic language" (Squires, 182). But this kind of criticism paints yet another fig leaf on the minds of first-time readers of this book. Phrases like "holy rites of intercourse" in literary criticism give to sex what Lawrence called the 'uplift' taint: "If I use the taboo words, there is a reason. We shall never free the phallic reality from the uplift taint till we give it its own phallic language, and use the obscene words. The greatest blasphemy of all against the phallic reality is this 'lifting it to a higher plane' " ("A Propos," 358).

Lawrence wants to wake us up with his language, to shock us, but not shock us into conforming to the ideal of "good sex" or humanism or to have us use such words with show-off bravado; rather, he wants to shock us away from our society's ideas on what good sex is and back to reality. He wants to shake the fig leaf out of our minds. "Balance up the consciousness of the act, and the act itself. Get the two in harmony. It means having a proper reverence for sex, and a proper awe of the body's strange experience. It means being able to use the so-called obscene words, because these are a natural part of the mind's consciousness and body. Obscenity only comes in when the mind despises and fears the body, and the body hates and resists the mind" ("A Propos," 333).

Balancing the sex act with the consciousness of it, the body with the mind, is a good description of one of the themes of the novel, and it is a good idea to keep this in mind when answering a question that often comes up in the classroom: What's the matter with everybody in the first seven chapters of this book? What's the matter with them, according to Lawrence, is that they haven't got a "proper reverence for sex" or a "proper awe of the body's strange experiences" ("A Propos," 333).

What must be understood about Lawrence's use of the English language, then, as we finish reading the first seven chapters, is that words like *glory, honor, courage, love,* and *sex,* and our famous "four-letter" words, will be put to use by the people at Wragby Hall in a way that is far different from the way they are put to use by Connie and Mellors in later chapters.

Modern Love

The relationship between Connie and Clifford was not very good to begin with. Before he was shipped off to war, the "sex part" of their marriage "did not mean much" to Clifford (*LCL,* 9). When he returns, crippled and unable to give Connie a child, their relationship continues much as we would have expected. Clifford is not in touch with anybody, not Connie, the coal miners in his mines, or his friends. His only interests are in Wragby Hall, in becoming a known writer, and perhaps in his sister, Emma. Under Tommy Dukes's questioning Clifford reveals his attitude toward sexuality:

> "Do you think sex is a dynamo to help a man on to success in the world?"

> Clifford rarely talked much at these times. He never held forth; his ideas were really not vital enough for it, he was too confused and emotional. Now he blushed and looked uncomfortable.
>
> "Well!" he said, "being myself *hors de combat,* I don't see I've anything to say on the matter."
>
> "Not at all," said Dukes; "the top of you's by no means *hors de combat.* You've got the life of the mind sound and intact. So let us hear your ideas."
>
> "Well," stammered Clifford, "even then I don't suppose I have much idea . . . I suppose marry-and-have-done-with-it would pretty well stand for what I think." (*LCL,* 34)

We understand by his remarks that Clifford hardly sees sex as important to marriage or as vital to the feelings between men and women. Lawrence is often criticized for making Clifford a sexless cripple (thereby making it easier for Connie to look for satisfaction elsewhere), a disembodied "symbol," whose wheelchair crushes flowers as he wheels himself into the woods to think up ways to improve the efficiency of England's new "machine-like" coal-mining industry. Lawrence answers these charges pretty well in "A Propos of *Lady Chatterley's Lover*":

> As to whether the "symbolism" is intentional—I don't know. Certainly not in the beginning, when Clifford was created. When I created Clifford and Connie, I had no idea what they were or why they were. They just came, pretty much as they are. But the novel was written, from start to finish, three times. And when I read the first version, I recognized that the lameness of Clifford was symbolic of the paralysis, the deeper emotional or passional paralysis, of most men of his sort and class today. I realized that it was perhaps taking an unfair advantage of Connie, to paralyse him technically. It made it so much more vulgar of her to leave him. Yet the story came as it did, by itself, so I left it alone. ("A Propos," 358)

Clifford's paralysis and coldness takes its toll on Connie in the first part of the novel, culminating in the mirror scene in chapter 7. Her body feels flat to her, meaningless, thin, with no relation to anything truly warm and freshening. "The mental life!" Connie thinks, "she hated it with a rushing fury, the swindle!" (73). The mental life at Wragby, the endless dry conversations about modern life, and Clifford's extraction of tribute from her for his clever and spiteful stories, "curiously true to modern life" though they be, were all filling Connie with a deep rebellion. People were noting a change in her, too. Her father comments in front of Clifford that he hopes "circumstance" will not force her into becoming a "*demi-vierge*," a half-virgin. "She's getting thin . . . angular. It's not her style," he says. "She's not the pilchard sort of little slip of a girl, she's a bonny Scotch trout" (15). And her sister, Hilda, forces Clifford to let her drive Connie to London so a doctor can examine her. Lawrence's intention in these opening chapters is to let us experience, in our *minds*, the stale mental life at Wragby, and to empathize, with our *feelings*, with Connie's needs.

Longing for something more substantial and vital, Connie's relationship with Michaelis is her first attempt at trying to find something real. Beneath his hang-dog expression and decision not to take his love making with Connie "personally," however, was a "child's soul . . . sobbing with gratitude" (27). Michaelis is a "trembling excited sort of lover, whose crisis soon came, and was finished . . . childlike" (27). The external man that he was, all cunning and wit, perfectly adaptable to the modern world, was not the internal man. The inner man was passive. Like all his generation, Lawrence says, he was "hopeless at the very core," and Connie felt the "reflection of his hopelessness" in her. She couldn't love "in hopelessness." "And he, being hopeless, couldn't ever quite love at all" (28). Still, she wanted the sexual, mental thrill she could get from him, and she felt she could love him, to even agree to his abrupt and self-centered marriage proposal. "I can give a woman the darndest good time she can ask for," he said (54). All of this comes crashing down at the end of chapter 5. Clifford's giving himself over to the "bitch-goddess" of success had come to nothing but a display, Connie realized, and it turned out that Michaelis was even better at making such a "display of nothingness" (52). Both were sexless men, whose biggest need was not making money but making a show of themselves in order to capture England's attention. Michaelis kills off Connie's feelings for him with this speech:

"You couldn't go off at the same time as a man, could you? You'd have to bring yourself off! You'd have to run the show!"

This little speech, at the moment, was one of the shocks of her life. Because that passive sort of giving himself was so obviously his only real mode of intercourse. . . .

"All the darned women are like that," he said. "Either they don't go off at all, as if they were dead in there . . . or else they wait till a chap's really done, and then they start in to bring themselves off, and a chap's got to hang on. I never had a woman yet who went off just at the same moment as I did. . . ."

This speech was one of the crucial blows of Connie's life. It killed something in her. . . . Her whole sexual feeling for him, or for any man, collapsed that night. (*LCL*, 55–56)

Michaelis's behavior toward Connie is Lawrence's illustration of the drawing-room theories touted by Clifford's friends in chapter 4. Hopelessness characterizes the discussion of Dukes, May, Hammond, Berry, and Clifford. Their talk of sexuality and politics reflects what Dukes calls a "mental friction," a spitefulness of the mind. Once we start living the "mental life," he says, we "pluck the apple." We sever the "connection between the apple and the tree: the organic connection." And if we've got nothing "*but* the mental life," then it is logical that we would be spiteful (37). Dukes says much the same thing about forcing political ideals into a practical system—whether the "Soviet-social thing" or the whole industrial ideal of free enterprise. Hate is the product of both systems. Berry asks Dukes if he believes in love at all, then, and Dukes's response represents Lawrence's description of modern love:

"Fellows with swaying waists fucking little jazz girls with small-boy buttocks, like two collar studs! Do you mean that sort of love? Or the joint-property, make-a-success-of-it, My-husband-my-wife sort of love? No, my fine fellow, I don't believe in it at all!"

"But you do believe in something?"

"Me? Oh, intellectually I believe in having a good heart, a chirpy penis, a lively intelligence, and the courage to say 'shit!' in front of a lady." (*LCL*, 39–40)

Connie has been listening to this conversation, and she is "infinitely amused" by it. "She had an immense respect for thought . . . and these men, at least, tried to think honestly. But somehow there was a cat, and it wouldn't jump. They all alike talked at something, though what it was, for the life of her she couldn't say. It was something that Mick didn't clear, either" (36). She retorts: "There are nice women in the world," but the men resented hearing that. Dukes concludes that it's all hopeless, and Berry maintains that to remain pure is the cure— "It's much less complicated" (40). It is important for us as readers of *Lady Chatterley's Lover* that we understand more fully Lawrence's ideas on modern love, so that we may appreciate the message he is trying to send to us in his descriptions of the relationship between Connie and Mellors.

D. H. Lawrence defined modern love as the man getting the "better of a woman, in the sexual intercourse; the self-seeking, automatic civilized man trying to extend his ego over a woman"; and it is the woman, "putting her will over him, and thereby getting a sense of power and enlargement in herself."[4] As a result, the "strange, tender flow of sex" shuts off, and so the women, eventually tired and fed up with the struggle to dominate, leave the men to "fight for the money," while they fight for other men. "This is called love. 'She is terribly in love with him,' that cant phrase means really: 'she is mad to get him under her will' " (*JTLJ*, 106). Virginia Woolf describes this pattern of behavior in her novel *Between the Acts,* between Giles, the stockbroker who tried the search for money and status and got tired of it, and his wife, Isa.[5]

Lawrence shows us Connie, too, "in love" with Michaelis, tiring of money, status, marital domination, and sexual acquisition, and gaining, for a time, a way out of modern love's conscious, acquisitive behavior. Yet it is not Connie who is the solution to our modern ennui about sex, nor is it Mellors, the mouthpiece for Lawrence's own idealism; it is instead the relationship between them. Over the years so many critics have made the mistake of seeing Lawrence's solutions to our troubles in the behavior of either Connie or Mellors. By doing this they overlook what Lawrence said about the relationship itself: that it is the "tremble of life" that exists apart from the egos of his characters.

And what makes up the relationship is the bodies of the characters, in sexual desire, appearing to us as what we often know them to be in real life: strangers to our cerebral selves. Instead of contriving symbol or myth to remind us of our sexual passions, as does Woolf in *Between the Acts* and James Joyce in *Ulysses,* Lawrence shows us our concrete sexual desires.

One particular moment in *Lady Chatterley's Lover* illustrates what Lawrence meant by desire. Drawn down into the woods to get away from Clifford's theories on the thrill of thought and the conquest of touch, Connie makes her way toward the gamekeeper's hut and crouches in front of a chicken coop. She begins to feed the pheasant chicks, crouched among the little birds, crying.

> The keeper squatting beside her, was also watching with an amused face the bold little bird in her hands. Suddenly he saw a tear fall on to her wrist.
>
> And he stood up, and stood away, moving to the other coop. For suddenly he was aware of the old flame shooting and leaping up in his loins, that he had hoped was quiescent for ever. He fought against it, turning his back to her. But it leapt, and leapt downwards, circling in his knees.
>
> He turned again to look at her. She was kneeling and holding her two hands slowly forward, blindly, so that the chicken should run in to the mother hen again. And there was something so mute and forlorn in her, compassion flamed in his bowels for her.
>
> Without knowing, he came quickly towards her and crouched beside her again, taking the chick from her, because she was afraid of the hen, and putting it back in the coop. At the back of his loins the fire suddenly darted stronger.
>
> He glanced apprehensively at her. Her face was averted, and she was crying blindly, in all the anguish of her generation's forlornness. His heart melted suddenly, like a drop of fire, and he put out his hand and laid his fingers on her knee.
>
> "You shouldn't cry," he said softly.
>
> But then she put her hands over her face and felt that really her heart was broken and nothing mattered any more.
>
> He laid his hand on her shoulder, and softly, gently, it began to travel down the cure of her back, blindly, with a blind

stroking motion, to the curve of her crouching loins. And there
his hand softly, softly, stroked the curve of her flank, in the blind
instinctive caress. (*LCL*, 122–23)

There is such a glowing lambency in this scene, a delicate, unconscious, and powerful sense of desire. The scene is a rebuttal to our
popular ideas about the ennui of modern love, with its talkiness and
suffering. The yielding of these two characters to each other is not
expected by them, or courted by them, and the unconscious nature of
it is made all the more curiously necessary in our eyes because
Lawrence does not spell out its meaning.[6] He allows the emotional
details to speak for themselves, thus lowering as much as possible our
barriers of aesthetic distance. For it is here, in scenes like these, that
aesthetic experience becomes human experience. The scene communi-
cates the impersonality and submerged nature of sexual desire, of our
senses' tender. And since our belief about the ennui of modern love is
challenged by *Lady Chatterley's Lover* and our aesthetic distance difficult to maintain, we often resist what we read or call it unreal or
ridiculous, not possible at all in our iron world.

Our traditional views about unfulfilled love are upheld by a conventional novel, and our traditional despair over the conventional
tragedy of a loveless world is often applauded. "This is the ugly fact
which underlies our civilization. As the advertisement of one of the
war novels said, it is an epic of 'friendship and hope, mud and blood,'
which means, of course, that the friendship and hope must end in mud
and blood" ("A Propos," 356). Not so for a Lawrence novel. *Lady
Chatterley's Lover* does not end in "mud and blood."

In stark contrast to the mental life at Wragby, and to our
world's modern love, is Lawrence's wood. Every time there is a statement on love, work, and success at Wragby, there is a counterscene,
as it were, in the wood, a scene to battle the hopeless thoughts of
Clifford's friends. At first reading, the novel appears to be a debate
between two opposing but tired forces: the wood, with its center of
vital and growing but vulnerable life, and Wragby Hall, the emblem
of modern thought, industry, hopelessness, and mental friction. But
things are a little more complicated than that. One day, Clifford

wheels his theories about love and lineage into the wood, and makes it clear to Connie that he wants an heir to his property and name; he makes it equally clear that he doesn't care about fatherhood or, as we've read earlier, about sexual love. But he does believe tradition is important, the tradition of England as *he* represents England. Fate has given him a cruel blow, since his war injuries have left him impotent. So why not, he asks Connie, "arrange this sex thing, as we arrange going to the dentist"? Isn't it true, he asks, that sex should be subordinated to preserving the long life they will live together? Connie responds that she may agree, now, but that "life may turn quite a new face" on that theory. And indeed it does, and at precisely this moment, for out of the wood emerges Mellors, the gamekeeper, with a "swift menace." Connie sees him as a "threat out of nowhere," a danger that will undermine Clifford's theories (45–46). Then, in one of the supreme ironies of the novel, Mellors is asked to push Clifford in his motorized wheelchair up a hill and back to the house (an episode that will be repeated in chapter 13). Here we have a strong young man, with an active mind, someone who has power over other men and who has achieved a little fame as a writer, trapped in a wheelchair, and dependent on a wife who must lift the burden of his dead legs in and out of the chair. He must be helped by a somewhat frail man, who, surviving World War I, has power over no one, who lives alone and likes it that way, and is interested in neither fame nor fortune. Yet he is someone who Connie feels from the first is potent and dangerous.

As Connie listens to Clifford's description of Mellors's personal background, about his days as a miner in Tevershall, his exwife, Bertha, his mother and daughter, she sees in her husband's eyes a peculiar "nothingness." In one of the key passages in the first seven chapters of the novel, Lawrence tells us what Connie realizes about this "nothingness": "And dimly she realized one of the great laws of the human soul: that when the emotional soul receives a wounding shock, which does not kill the body, the soul seems to recover as the body recovers. But this is only appearance. It is really only the mechanism of the re-assumed habit. Slowly, slowly the wound to the soul begins to make itself felt, like a bruise, which only slowly deepens its terrible ache, till it fills all the psyche. And when we think we have recovered and forgotten, it is then that the terrible after-effects have to be encountered at their worst" (*LCL*, 50). All of the characters in *Lady Chatterley's Lover* suffer from a modern wounding of one kind or another, especially Clifford, Connie, Dukes, and Mellors, and it will be the working out of "the terrible after-effects" of this wounding that Connie and Mellors will have to endure, each in their own way, as Dukes and Mrs. Bolton have worked through theirs.

THE LAWRENCE "CHARACTER"

Before we discuss further the relationships between these characters and the way they work through their woundings, we need to look at Lawrence's concept of *character* itself, and then discuss each important "character" in the novel.

Traditional commentary has it that there are three ways for an author to present a character in a novel: (1) by direct commentary on traits before the character is presented in action; (2) by descriptions of characters in action only, so that readers will deduce what the person is like; and (3) by a character's inner dialogue, given to the reader without a lot of commentary by the author. In all his novels, but especially in *Sons and Lovers* and *Lady Chatterley's Lover,* Lawrence uses the first of these techniques. For example, in the opening paragraphs of *Lady Chatterley's Lover,* we read that Connie was a "ruddy, country-looking girl with soft brown hair and sturdy body, and slow movements. . . . She had big, wondering eyes," and from an early age she was "not the least daunted by either art or ideal politics" (*LCL*, 2). Authorial commentary on Mellors's character is plain and direct: "He cherished his solitude as his only and last freedom in life" (*LCL*, 91). In fact, all of the characters in the novel are described forthrightly and plainly before, during, and after any action that might be used to further the plot. Lawrence deliberately comments on character traits, summarizes the inner thoughts and feelings of his characters, and only once, in a big way, does he leave the inner dialogue of a character alone: when he closes the novel with Mellors's letter to Connie.

The novel is a traditional one, really, in form, with introductions, set-pieces of action, and a plot line that leads to something of a final act. It is important to remember, however, that after seeing *The Rainbow* banned early in his life and witnessing his poems and paintings seized by the London police during his last years, Lawrence had decided to abandon the experimentation with character development he took up in *The Rainbow* and *Women in Love* and write a plain and simple novel for the public—a novel that also got him into trouble. And yet traces of his early experimentation with character remain in *Lady Chatterley's Lover*. It is vital that we understand Lawrence's new concept of character, for it figures largely even in what might appear to be rather conventional actions and dialogues between Connie and Mellors in the middle of the book. Our text must now bear the brunt of a lengthy quote, a letter Lawrence wrote to Edward Garnet, dated 5 June 1914, for it is one of the most important letters he ever wrote. (I have italicized particularly important phrases that are germane to the discussion that follows.)

Lawrence describes what he is attempting to do in *The Rainbow* and *Women in Love* this way:

> I think [*The Rainbow*] is a bit futuristic—quite unconsciously so. But when I read Marinetti—"The profound intuitions of life added one to the other, word by word, according to their illogical conception, will give us the general lines of an intuitive physiology of matter"—I see something of what I am after . . . I don't care about physiology of matter—but somehow—that which is physic—*non-human, in humanity, is more interesting to me than the old-fashioned human element*—which causes one to conceive a character in a certain moral scheme and make him consistent. The certain moral scheme is what I object to. . . . When Marinetti writes: "It is the solidity of a blade of steel that is interesting by itself, that is, the incomprehending and inhuman alliance of its molecules in resistance to, let us say, a bullet. The heat of a piece of wood or iron is in fact more passionate, for us, than the laughter or tears of a woman"—then I know what he means. He is stupid, as an artist, for contrasting the heat of the iron and the laugh of the woman. Because what is interesting in the laugh of the

woman is the same as the binding of the molecules of steel or their action in heat: *it is the inhuman will, call it physiology,* or like Marinetti—*physiology of matter, that fascinates me.* I don't care so much about what the woman *feels*—in the ordinary usage of the word. That presumes an *ego* [italics in original] to feel with. *I only care about what the woman is—what she is—inhumanly, physiologically, materially*—according to the use of the word: but for me, what she *is* as a phenomenon (or as representing some greater, inhuman will) . . . *You mustn't look in my novel for the old stable ego of the character. There is another ego, according to whose action the individual is unrecognizable,* and passes through, as it were, allotropic states . . . to discover . . . the same single radically-unchanged element. Again, I say, don't look for the development of the novel to follow the lines of certain characters: the *characters fall into the form of some other rhythmic form,* like when one draws a fiddle-bow across a fine tray delicately sanded, the sand takes lines unknown. (*Letters,* 2:181–84)

What Lawrence says here about character is completely new in the history of English fiction. He is attempting, as best he can, to leave behind traditional descriptions of characters in action by showing us what his characters do without a lot of commentary. He wants us to understand that his characters, in *Women in Love,* for example, and in *Lady Chatterley's Lover,* choose their own fates from their own psychic demands, and not *exclusively* from social pressures or forces. In other words, there are "nonhuman," essential, and basic elements in human beings that compel them to change, or even look for the nonhuman in those they love. That's why Lawrence said we shouldn't look for characters who develop along the lines of traditional characterization (as outlined above); rather, we should look in his novels for characters that have a new rhythmic form, "as when one draws a fiddle-bow across a fine tray delicately sanded, and sand takes lines unknown." What does Lawrence mean by this? Perhaps he is suggesting that the fiddle-bow, held by himself as the novelist, is playing the tray of sand, his novel, and that this fiddle-bow represents all of *his* own psychic demands. Or perhaps he is suggesting that the sand represents his characters, who say and do what they find themselves saying

and doing as they discover how they react to *their* own needs, as fil-
tered through Lawrence's psychic demands.

This is not to say that *Women in Love* and *Lady Chatterley's
Lover* are purely autobiographical novels. *Lady Chatterley's Lover* is a
novel, not a diary. Yet when Lawrence is criticized for failing to
achieve some ideal theory of form or characterization that academic
critics have in mind, when, for example, it is said that although
Lawrence "has devised a new vocabulary for describing the essence of
character he has not supported the intense inner vision with forms of
action that would express it with inevitable fitness,"[7] then Lawrence
must answer his critics quite plainly and patiently in the following
way; and his answer here could be a description of his characterization
in *Women in Love* as well as in *Lady Chatterley's Lover*. "This novel
pretends only to be a record of the writer's own desires, aspirations,
struggles; in a word, a record of the profoundest experiences in the
self. Nothing that comes from the deep, passional soul is bad, or can
be bad. So there is no apology to tender, unless to the soul itself, if it
should have been belied. . . . This struggle for verbal consciousness
should not be left out in art. It is a very great part of life. It is not
superimposition of a theory. It is the passionate struggle into conscious
being."[8] This Lawrence says about himself in his foreword to *Women
in Love,* and since Lawrence's novels, especially *Lady Chatterley's
Lover,* are records of characters who also engage in a "passionate
struggle into conscious being," then it is hardly likely that Lawrence's
rhythmic form could ever have anything at all to do with academia's
"inevitable fitness."

With all of this in mind, let's look at some of the characters in
Lady Chatterley's Lover to see if we can find in them that rhythmic
form of their elemental, "inhuman will."

Sir Clifford Chatterley   As we know from the text, Clifford is
the owner of an estate at Wragby, in the Midlands of England.
Descended from an old aristocratic family, and rather disdainful of
sexual matters, he is wounded during World War I at Flanders and is
shipped home permanently paralyzed and impotent. He will spend the
rest of his days in a wheelchair, unable to give Connie children and left

only to study the engineering of coal mining and engage in parlor talk with his friends. Lawrence does engage a little of our sympathy for this character in the beginning of the novel, with descriptions such as this: "he could drive himself slowly round the garden and into the fine melancholy park, of which he was really so proud"; "Having suffered so much, the capacity for suffering had to some extent left him . . . he had been so much hurt that something inside him had perished, some of his feelings had gone" (*LCL,* 2); "Poor Clifford, he was not to blame. His was the greater misfortune. . . . It was all part of the general catastrophe" (*LCL,* 74). And yet we are never to forget that Clifford was aristocracy. He was secure in this narrow world, but quite uncomfortable in the world of "middle and lower classes" (*LCL,* 7). He possessed a superficial rebellion against authority that riches and comfort made possible, and on one occasion, when his brother, Herbert, later killed in the war, laughed outright at their father's "determined patriotism," a patriotism that cut down Wragby trees for trench props and weeded men out of the coal mines in order to "shove them into the war," Clifford could only smile "a little uneasily" (*LCL,* 7). The fact of the matter is that for Lawrence, Clifford remained the snob, with his British stiff upper lip intact, determined to get an heir to the Wragby throne. We are presented with the rhythmic form of Clifford's "inhuman will" in a decidedly negative light.

Even before his paralysis, we are told, Clifford thought sex to be "not really necessary," and it is this belief that characterizes his actions and conversations throughout the novel. Like his friends May and Hammond in chapter 4, Clifford believes in the life of the mind (*LCL,* 31), and the mind, for Hammond, as well as sex, should serve the interests of property, self-assertion, and success. May believes in pursuing any woman he likes, and since marriage to him would "stultify" his mind, he sees sleeping with a woman as "just an interchange of sensations instead of ideas" (*LCL,* 32). When Clifford is asked what he thinks, he blushes and stammers, and announces that sex should perfect the mental intimacy between men and women (*LCL,* 34), which he later explains in chapter 5 as the "habit" of living together. "It's the living together from day to day," he says to Connie, "not the sleeping together once or twice. You and I are married, no matter what happens to us. We have the habit of each other. And habit, to my thinking, is more vital than any occasional excitement" (*LCL*, 44–45). The real secret of marriage for Clifford is not sex but a "sort of unison," an intricate "vibration" between two people. With this disembodied view of life, Clifford finds it easy, then, to tell Connie that if she were to become pregnant by another man he would be pleased, for his heir would be only a "link in a chain" that would preserve the tradition of England: ownership and preservation of property. "You just wouldn't let the wrong sort of fellow touch you," he tells Connie (*LCL*, 45). There is something terribly cold in Clifford's practical advice here; his rhythmic form as a character is "hard and separate, and warmth to [him] was just bad taste" (*LCL*, 74). What is in good taste for Clifford is fully explored in chapter 13, where we are shown his inhuman will in all of its strange and modern purpose.

The chapter opens with Lawrence once again getting us to feel a little sympathy for Clifford: "It was cruel for Clifford, while the world bloomed, to have to be helped from chair to bath-chair" (*LCL*, 192). Yet any such feeling on our part is quickly dispensed with: he "seemed to have a certain conceit of himself in his lameness" (*LCL*, 192). Clifford decides to go into the woods in his motorized wheelchair, his "foaming steed," he jokingly calls it, and as he comes "puffing along" the drive in front of his estate he says, "I ride upon the achievements of the mind of man, and that beats a horse" (*LCL*, 192). Whether he is joking again or whether he is serious is not clear; nevertheless, he presents a pathetic sight. As Connie walks next to him, the conversation between them turns serious, and we begin to fully understand the nature of Clifford's view of the modern world and how such a world should be ordered. Connie supports the right of coal miners to strike for better wages and believes that Clifford should, too. But Clifford disagrees, claiming that since "industry fills their bellies" they should be content.

> "But didn't you say the other day that you were a conservative-anarchist," she asked innocently.
> "And did you understand what I meant?" he retorted. "All I meant is, people can be what they like and feel what they like

and do what they like, strictly privately, so long as they keep the *form* of life intact, and the apparatus. (*LCL,* 193)

In other words, for Clifford, people should conform to the prevailing structure of the world they find themselves living within, and not tear down the scaffolding that supports a working economic model. Connie responds by asking if the working man will let men like Clifford dictate terms, and if there simply can't be mutual understanding. Clifford answers that if the terms are gently dictated, they will have to submit, and only when they realize that "industry comes before the individual" (*LCL,* 194) can there be understanding between bosses and workers. There are only two classes in Clifford's world: rulers and workers; and the workers, the masses, are not men but animals, who remain unchanged as a group, no matter how many people emerge or escape from the group (*LCL,* 196).

> Aristocracy is a function, a part of fate. And the masses are a functioning of another part of fate. . . . The individual hardly matters. It is a question of which function you are brought up to and adapted to. It is not the individuals that make an aristocracy: it is the functioning of the aristocratic whole. And it is the functioning of the whole mass that makes the common man what he is. . . . But when it comes to expressive or executive functioning, I believe there is a gulf and an absolute one, between the ruling and the serving classes. The two functions are opposed. And the function determines the individual. (*LCL,* 197)

For Clifford, then, the social and economic function a man serves defines the essence of his individuality, and, like the mine owner Gerald Crich in *Women in Love,* Clifford believes in the "pure instrumentality of mankind."[9]

Gerald Crich and Clifford Chatterley are very similar characters, and many of Clifford's beliefs were first defined by Lawrence in the chapter titled "The Industrial Magnate" from *Women in Love.* Like Clifford, Gerald set himself to get "the great industry" in order to fight "with the earth and the coal" and "reduce it to his will" (*WIL,* 301). The rhythmic form of Gerald's "inhuman will" is his obsession with efficiency, smoothness, and the reduction of men to mechanical duties. He established in his mines, as Clifford wanted to do, "a great and perfect machine, a system, an activity of pure order, pure mechanical repetition," all to give expression to his will and life to his power (*WIL,* 301). This establishment of will and power is implied in Clifford's half-joke to Connie: that in his wheelchair, with its little motor, he rides "upon the achievements of the mind of man" (*LCL,* 192). In Gerald's mine, everything "was run on the most accurate and delicate scientific method, educated and expert men were in control everywhere" (*WIL,* 304). And the miners themselves submitted to the power of such a system, partly because they had no choice, but also because they were lured by it, and in awe of it. "There was a new world, a new order, strict, terrible, inhuman, but satisfying in its very destructiveness. The men were satisfied to belong to the great and wonderful machine, even whilst it destroyed them. It was what they wanted. It was the highest that man had produced, the most wonderful and superhuman . . . beyond feeling or reason, something really godlike. Their hearts died within them, but their souls were satisfied" (*WIL,* 304). Clifford Chatterley and Gerald Crich's new world order (not much different from our own) is the satisfaction men get in submitting to their own destruction after being promised by their "leaders" that a new, more wonderful, yet fake utopia is just around the corner. In *Women in Love,* Gerald's subjection of life to mechanical principles leads to his death; in *Lady Chatterley's Lover,* however, Clifford lives to be brutally satirized, in the remaining pages of chapter 13.

The wheelchair, puffing and plugging slowly through the woods and crushing flowers wherever it goes, breaks down. The engine, the instrument of Clifford's will and the symbol of his utopian plans, gives out. What follows in six long pages is both a painful comedy and a serious comment on the sterility of the human will as it tries to subdue organic nature by purely mechanical means. When the chair stops with "curious noises," like "a sick thing," Clifford is determined to get it started again. Connie wants to push him, but he angrily denies her, and only after repeated attempts to start the engine does he honk the little horn he has attached to the chair so that Mellors might come and help. They both wait for Mellors, in silence. A "wood-pigeon began to coo, roo-hoo hoo! roo-hoo, hoo!" Like an exasperated idealist who is suddenly reminded of the complexities of reality, Clifford shuts the bird up "with a blast on the horn." When Mellors arrives, Clifford asks him to take a look at the engine, but Mellors knows nothing about them. He crawls under the chair and pokes around, but he finds nothing. Clifford yells at Mellors not to push him, and then violently jabs at the levers, running the engine faster and faster. Fighting the hill, the chair suddenly lurches and threatens to topple over into a ditch. Mellors grabs the arm rail and then pushes from behind, but Clifford snarls at him to let go. Both Connie and Mellors now stand back and watch, as Clifford, through the sheer force of his will and with "savage impatience," jerks at the levers to no avail. Connie sits down and repeats to herself with irony the fragments of Clifford's description of the new world order: "I can do my share of ruling." "What we need to take up now is whips, not swords." "The ruling classes!" (*LCL*, 203).

Finally, after Clifford admits the machine has given out, he asks Mellors to push him home. Connie learns, as do we, that the rhythmic form of Clifford's inhuman will is the negative bullying of his belief in mechanical power. He is a bully, with his money, and as he sits there, in his living room, he appears to her what he finally has become: "a skeleton, sending out a skeleton's cold grizzly *will* against her" (*LCL*, 209).

Connie Chatterley   To be sure, Connie, the daughter of Sir Malcolm Reid, is a member of Clifford's "ruling class"; if not a full blue-blooded aristocrat, she is a member of the "well-to-do-intelligentsia" (*LCL*, 6). And yet we know from Lawrence's first descriptions of her that she is different, not at all like the wives of Clifford's friends or even her sister, Hilda. We can safely say that she is Lawrence's lead character in this novel, not only because most of the action in the novel is seen through her eyes but also because as a character she illustrates most clearly Lawrence's new theory of character—that there is "another ego, according to whose action the individual is unrecognizable, and passes through, as it were, allotropic states" toward a deeper level or state, toward what is inhuman, physiological, material. Connie is first described as a "ruddy, country-looking girl," with "slow movements" and "full of unusual energy"

(*LCL*, 2). We learn that Connie's "energy" is really an eagerness for life and that the slow development of the rhythmic form of her elemental, inhuman will is decidedly positive.

As a young women of 18, Connie is described by Lawrence as a modern "girl," cosmopolitan, at ease with ideal politics, supremely free, and annoyed in her love affairs if boys trespass on her "inner freedom" (*LCL*, 3). "The beautiful pure freedom of a woman was infinitely more wonderful than any sexual love" (*LCL*, 4). Connie would take a man without giving herself to him and use sex to have power over her boy. More important than sex was talk, to be able to passionately talk to a "really clever young man by the hour" (*LCL*, 4). Sent to Dresden for their education, both Hilda and Connie had "tramped off to the forests" with sturdy German boys "bearing guitars, twang-twang!" (*LCL*, 3), and their "discussions were the great thing: the love-making . . . a sort of primitive reversion and a bit of an anticlimax" (*LCL*, 3). But at the outbreak of World War I, with their German lovers quickly killed at the front, Connie and Hilda are whisked back home to Kensington. Connie marries Clifford in her mid-20s, and at this point in her life she is described as "so much more mistress of herself" in the real world than Clifford was "master of himself" (*LCL*, 7). The fact that Connie is, indeed, a mistress of herself explains her courage in facing her own unhappiness and growing restlessness with her position in life.

So much of Connie's character is delineated by the descriptions of her restlessness, her search for fulfillment, and her eventual angry rejection of her life. Like Ursula in *Women in Love,* Connie begins to feel a "tight horror, when it seemed to her that her life would pass away, and be gone, without having been more" (*WIL*, 103). She is getting thinner, she suffers from heart palpitations, and her father is worried about her. So she drifts into her affair with "Mick." But what she learns about her deeper character is that she cannot be satisfied with men like Michaelis or any of Clifford's friends, whose drawing-room conversations were filled with spite, hopelessness about modern life, and money. Breaking through the crust of her modern character, her personality, is another Connie, a Connie different from the modern girl Lawrence described in the opening chapters. In chapter 6, Connie discovers that she likes the *"inwardness"* of the forest (*LCL*, 67), that the silence of the wood somehow speaks to something in her, and that in the wood, around trees, she seems to find what her deeper character felt to be a "proper destiny" (*LCL*, 90). And after seeing Mellors fix a chicken coop, she suddenly realizes that she is drawn to the idea that Mellors is like "an animal that works alone," a "soul that recoils." He was "patient and withdrawn," as she needed to be, and this new desire "relieved her of herself" so that a new, more essential Connie could emerge (*LCL*, 92–93).

A good deal of Connie's early character is made up of those things that give her mental excitement: drawing-room conversations, art, politics, the preservation of her will. But the "mental excitement had worn itself out" (*LCL*, 101), and she will, by chapter 10, flee as much as possible into the wood. Slowly, by degrees, Connie's elemental inhuman qualities take on a life of their own, underneath her personality, even though after giving herself to Mellors she asks "Why was this necessary? Was it real?" (*LCL*, 124). "Men were very kind to the *person* she was, but rather cruel to the female, despising her or ignoring her altogether. Men were awfully kind to Constance Reid or to Lady Chatterley; but not to her womb they weren't kind" (*LCL*, 129). Despite the fact that Connie did not really *like* Mellors, especially when she reminded herself that he was, after all, "working class," she still felt that she needed a man who was kind to her as a *female*. Yet Connie's personality resented the fact that Mellors had lumped her "together with all the rest of his female womanhood in his 'thee' and 'tha' " (*LCL*, 137). Connie's "individuality" was insulted. When they make love for the second time in chapter 10, however, after Mellors leads Connie through the trees to a little space, Connie realizes that a very radical change has taken place inside her.

> Another self was alive in her, burning molten and soft in her womb and bowels, and with this self she adored him . . . it made her feel she was very different from her old self, and as if she was sinking deep, deep to the centre of all womanhood and the sleep of creation . . . she feared it still, lest if she adored him too much, then she would lose herself, become effaced . . . a slave . . .

> So, in the flux of new awakening, the old hard passion
> flamed in her for a time, and the man dwindled to a contemptible
> object, the mere phallus-bearer, to be torn to pieces when his ser-
> vice was performed . . . but while she felt this, her heart was
> heavy. She did not want it, it was known and barren, birthless.
> (*LCL*, 143–44)

Here Connie has passed through Lawrence's "allotropic state" to find in herself the unchanging elements of creation. Her surface character has fallen into "some other rhythmic form," forged as it was in the deeper feelings of the body itself. A scene from *Women in Love* may help us further understand what this Other is, hiding under the surface of Lawrence's "characters":

> There were faint sounds from the wood, but no disturbance . . .
> the world was under a strange ban, a new mystery had super-
> vened. They threw off their clothes, and he gathered her to him,
> and found her, found the pure lambent reality of her forever
> invisible flesh. Quenched, inhuman, his fingers upon her unre-
> vealed nudity were the fingers of silence upon silence, the body of
> mysterious night upon the body of mysterious night, the night
> masculine and feminine, never to be seen with the eye, or known
> with the mind, only known as a palpable revelation of mystic oth-
> erness.
>   . . . It was already high day when he awoke. They looked at
> each other and laughed, then looked away, filled with darkness
> and secrecy . . . they were afraid to seem to remember. They hid
> away the remembrance and the knowledge. (*WIL*, 403)

These quotes are witness to Lawrence's struggle with the English language as he tries to get it to bend to his descriptions of this different, dark, and elemental Other in both men and women, in Ursula and Birkin above, and in Connie and Mellors in *Lady Chatterley's Lover*. What Connie learns, and what Lawrence tries to tell us, is that profound sexual experience reveals not the "personality," or "character," or even a "Connie," but the body, in complete otherness.

Of course, Connie's daily surface character changes, too: she is much more confident in her desire for Mellors by the time we read chapter 16, where she gives to Clifford her famous, "Give me the body" speech; and she is now more willing to fight for her fulfillment, despite her second thoughts and misgivings about Mellors. And after having her experiences with Mellors, she now sees that most people pursue narcotic effects in one way or another. When Connie travels to Paris with Hilda in chapter 17, she finds she can no longer enjoy herself in the usual social way: "jazzing with your stomach up against some fellow in the warm nights, cooling off with ices, it was a complete narcotic. And that was what they all wanted, a drug . . . the sun, a drug; jazz, a drug; cigarettes, cocktails, ices, vermouth. To be drugged!" (*LCL,* 281). Her sister, Hilda, who couldn't see much in Mellors, liked to "plaster her stomach" up to a man for a dance and then "break loose" from what she called "the creature." Connie couldn't do this at all. To her most if not all the men she saw were like dogs, "waiting to be patted" (*LCL,* 281).

Even more important to our understanding of how Connie's character has changed is how the change in the "bedrock" of her nature is described. After Mellors argues with Hilda in chapter 16, he makes love to Connie, only this time it was not the "thrills of tenderness" but a sharper, reckless sensuality that "shook" Connie "to her foundations . . . made a different woman of her." This time it wasn't love or voluptuousness, but something "sharp and searing as fire, burning the soul to tinder" (*LCL,* 267). And this time, in the last and most difficult change in Connie's "character," Lawrence describes what happens: "Shame, which is fear: the deep organic shame, the old, old physical fear which crouches in the bodily roots of us, and can only be chased away by the sensual fire, at last it was roused up and routed by the phallic hunt of the man, and she came to the very heart of the jungle of herself. She felt, now, she had come to the real bedrock of her nature, and was essentially shameless" (*LCL,* 268).

And because Connie felt shameless, because she felt that what she really wanted was a man who could give this "consuming, rather awful sensuality" without shame or misgiving, she refuses to give up on Mellors, or betray him, or deny how she has changed—even after hearing about the details of his marriage with Bertha Coutts and thinking that Mellors was, after all, "really common" (*LCL,* 286). Terrified of what her social circle might think of her, Connie would even crave the "utter respectability" of her past life. In the end, however, she does not go back on Mellors, or on what they have together.

Oliver Mellors   We know right away that Mellors is the game-keeper at the Wragby estate, but we really don't find out anything about him until chapter 10, when he gives us a few details himself. He tells us that he was a boy in Tevershall (or, as Mrs. Bolton puts it, "A Tevershall lad born and bred" [*LCL,* 155]), that he was married "five or six years" (to Bertha Coutts), and that he joined up in 1915 to serve as a soldier in India and Egypt. He received the rank of lieutenant, damaged his health, and then left the army "to be a working man again" (*LCL,* 150). Mrs. Bolton fills in some details for us, too, when we learn that in Tevershall, Mellors had helped her with her anatomy class. "He'd been a clever boy, had a scholarship from Sheffield Grammar School, and learned French and things: and then after all had become an overhead blacksmith shoeing horses, because he was fond of horses, he said: but really because he was frightened to go out and face the world, only he'd never admit it" (*LCL,* 154–55).

Mellors could even be called a "gentleman" on some accounts, despite his working-class background. He is after all educated, and having been an officer in the army is probably quite at ease with both common troops and elite officers. He comports himself well with Connie's father and is at ease in London's social circles. When Connie's father asks her where Mellors was born, she responds: "He was a collier's son in Tevershall. But he's absolutely presentable" (*LCL,* 305). And he is. Mellors *is* "presentable," despite Sir Malcolm's fear of the scandal more than the affair. For Mellors is a character who has learned how to adapt to the social pressure to conform, first, by switching from his dialect to the King's English when necessary, and second, by fleeing from such pressure in condemning both working-class preoccupation with money and the moneyed classes' need to enslave. "Well, young man," asks Connie's father, Sir Malcolm, "and what about my daughter? . . . You've got a baby in her all right." Mellors answers in language he would hardly use with Connie: "I have that honour!" (307). In the end, Connie's father likes him a great deal. "But you warmed her up, oh, you warmed her up, I can see that. Ha-ha! My blood in her! You set fire to her haystack all right . . . Gamekeeper! Christ, but it's rich. I like it! Oh, I like it! Shows the girl's got spunk" (*LCL,* 307–8). Yet Mellors remains the outsider, belonging neither socially nor politically to the working class or the upper class; and he is not lonely, either. For he is what Lawrence called an "aristocrat of the sun," drawing his "nobility" from the inward sun in himself: and since he is someone who does not measure himself by looking at other people, he does not need to be a "money-slave" or a "social worm" ("Aristocracy of the Sun," *Complete Poems,* 526).

What frees Mellors from becoming a clichéd character in a Victorian melodrama (the feeling brute who seduces the repressed maiden) is the fact that Lawrence gives him the sometime manners of a "gentle man" by fusing his Tevershall background to his life experiences in the army, in his first marriage, and in the wood as a gamekeeper. These experiences free his character from being pigeonholed as the working-class man—a narrow category so often used by academics in criticism describing him. When Connie and Mellors strip off their clothing in this novel, it is difficult for us to see their bodies or even their selves as "representatives" of their class—he the exploited son of a coal miner and she the spoiled member of the ruling class, despite the obvious resemblance to Lawrence and his wife, Frieda. Lawrence does not give us the character of Mellors, in what Scoot Sanders calls the "central fable" of *Lady Chatterley's Lover,* as the "representative of the labouring millions, the downtrodden, the silent and suffering lower orders, [who] meets that titled representative of the ruling class in a hut in the magical wood" (Sanders, 177). Rather, Lawrence's point is that nakedness reveals the actual man and the actual woman, in "rhythmic form" of deeper movements underneath the social constraints of class. It is not just coitus as a "political act, defying the totalitarian claims of the state" (Sanders, 176)—although strong arguments could be waged to prove that Connie and Mellors *are* reduced to only "political acts"—but rather, if we accept Lawrence's definition of character, then Connie and Mellors's love making can be seen as a personal act, a surrender to Lawrence's "inhuman will," a deeper and more dangerous challenge not only to the claims of the state but also to politics itself. Mellors finally comes to believe in the flame between himself and Connie (*LCL,* 327), not in political activity. And this flame is a "demon" to the state and to conventional and radical politics. For it is interested only in itself and in a partner who surrenders to it as well.

> Oh be a demon
> outside all class!
> If you're a woman
> or even an ass
> still be a demon
> beyond the mass!
> . . . .
> You're not altogether
> such a human bird,
> you're as mixed as the weather,
> not just a good turd,
> so shut up pie-jaw blether,
> let your demon be heard.
> ("Be a Demon!" *Complete Poems,* 563–64)

As a character, Mellors is indeed as "mixed as the weather," for he reflects many of Lawrence's own ambivalent and contradictory feelings about being the son of a coal miner. Like Mellors, a "Tevershall lad born and bred" (*LCL,* 155), Lawrence was an Eastwood lad, born and bred as the fourth child of Arthur Lawrence, a miner in the coal fields of Nottinghamshire. As a boy, Lawrence grew up poking fun at the upper classes, disliking them and feeling angry at their leisure and money. "Do you hear my Rolls Royce purr, as it glides away? / —I lick the cream off property! that's what it seems to say!" ("Lord Tennyson and Lord Melchett," *Complete Poems,* 664). And yet, at the same time, because of his bad health and inability to do hard manual labor, he must have flirted with the idea of having enough money to get him out of the little village of his birth, to be a success as a writer, if not quite the complete gentleman. Lawrence's love-hate feelings for his background needed a solution, a middle space where Lawrence could breathe and feel neither weighed down by his boyhood past nor eaten alive by the middle-class highbrows of the art world or the moneyed bosses of city work. He traveled all over the world looking for a space to live in between these two worlds, but finally returned to England toward the end of his life to face his real feelings for his native village. He did give Mellors, however, a place to hide, and made him not the English "gentleman" that Lawrence despised but a gentleman with balls. "When is a man not a man?" Lawrence asks, "When he's a gentleman . . . where does it come from, this lovely English voice / . . . It has neither heart nor bowels nor genitals ("The Gentleman," *Complete Poems*, 830–31). Mellors has much the same opinion:

> "Do you hate Clifford?" [Connie asks Mellors.]
>   "Hate him, no! I've met too many like him to upset myself hating him. I know beforehand I don't care for his sort, and I let it go at that."
>   "What is his sort?"
>   "Nay, you know better than I do. The sort of youngish gentleman a bit like a lady, and no balls . . . none of that spunky wild bit of a man in him . . . sort of tame." (*LCL*, 211–12)

Mellors is neither a full member of the working world from which he has escaped nor a full member of the middle-class club. He occupies that "country in between the colliery regions," with its lonely beauty ("Fragment," 817), and the city, that "sparkling electric Thing" (*LCL*, 127). The character of Mellors lives in Lawrence's "middle-space" between upper- and lower-class values, a hopeful creation that lives at least in a novel's redemptive world if not in Lawrence's self. What finally defines Mellors as a character is his hatred for both worlds—bourgeois and Bolshevist. Through Mellors, Lawrence has created a new minority:

> Now above all is the time for the minorities of men,
> those who are neither bourgeois nor bolshevist; but true to life,
> to gather and fortify themselves, in every class, in every country,
> in every race.
> ("Minorities in Danger," *Complete Poems*, 666)

Mellors has gathered himself together and fortified himself in the wood, his space for life, readying himself for a fight to preserve a new life. His fights, his criticisms of the working class, are as pointed as his criticisms of the middle classes. The "common people" have become too success conscious and worship too keenly the machine, while the English middle classes, "prigs with half a ball," are conceited and frightened of change, Mellors says in chapter 15. The rhythmic form of Mellors's character is one that pulses to a fight, a fight for life.

So much of Lawrence's own criticism of his native village is put into the character of Mellors that one might imagine the following description from Lawrence's "Autobiographical Fragment" to be lifted from Mellors's compassionate soliloquy at the end of *Lady Chatterley's Lover*: "And there they stand, at the street corners and the entry-ends, the rough lads I went to school with, men now, with smart daughters and bossy wives and cigarette-smoking lads of their own. There they stand, then . . . as if they had o selves any more: decent, patient, self-effacing sort of men, who have seen the war and the high-water-mark wages, and now are down again, under, completely under . . . poor with a hopeless outlook and a new and expensive world around them" (818).

And yet Mellors's feelings, as well as Lawrence's, are divided between critique and sympathy. Both feel how "welcome death would be / if first a man could have his full revenge / on our castrated society" ("Welcome Death," *Complete Poems,* 628). Yet both Mellors and Lawrence conclude that if "you make a revolution, make it for fun," not because you hate people or money. "Don't do it for the working classes / Do it so that we can all of us be little aristocracies on our / own / and kick our heels like jolly escaped asses" ("A Sane Revolution," *Complete Poems,* 517). If only men could dance, sing, swagger about, stay alive and frisky, says Mellors in his letter to Connie. Let "the mass be for ever pagan" (*LCL,* 326). But of course they're not, nor will they ever be, as Mellors knows. And this is why his character often gives in to feelings of hopelessness. Mellors has a "terrible mistrust of the future" (*LCL,* 299). Nevertheless, under fire from Connie's probing questions at the beginning of chapter 18, Mellors reveals a very important aspect of his character, an aspect that does seek its own hope on its own terms. It is true that Mellors finds a bit of hope in Connie and in the child in her womb, if not in a "future for humanity" (*LCL,* 300).

But what is even more important for a man like Mellors is that he must feel he has something to offer a woman other than sex. "I'm not just my lady's fucker, after all," he tells Connie (*LCL,* 300). What shapes that solitary independence in Mellors that Connie likes so much is the need in Mellors for meaning in his life. His life, he tells Connie, must do something and get somewhere, "inwardly at least, to keep us both fresh" (*LCL,* 300). He is not sure what that something might be, and there is no solution at the end of the novel. But he is sure of one thing: that in his "battle" against the forces of money, conformity, politics, and deadening work, he will find purpose to his life. He knows instinctively that if he "loses his deep sense of purposive, creative activity," he will feel lost. He knows that the "ultimate, greatest desire in men is this desire for great *purposive* activity" (*Unconscious,* 143).

Bertha Coutts, Mellors's first wife, offers a means of understanding another dimension of his character, particularly the kind of sexual relationship he desires. Most of what we know about Bertha is second- and sometimes third-hand information. Chapter 17 reveals a letter written by Mrs. Bolton, Clifford's nurse, to Connie that explains what Bertha did after she returned to Mellors's hut in the woods. Yet even this part of the story, we are told by Bolton, had been told to her by Mellors's mother. Chapter 14 reveals a great deal about Bertha, too, but we learn it from Mellors, after Connie asks him, "Why did you marry her? She was commoner than yourself" (*LCL* 215). In fact, the longest description of Mellors's feelings about sex and women is told to us by Mellors himself as he describes his years with Bertha. The novel gives us no reason to doubt that what we hear about Bertha from Mellors and Bolton is true. Bolton is a keen observer of human behavior, and Mellors would have no reason to lie. Through his descriptions of Bertha we learn more about Mellors as a character— important information for us to have, since Lawrence cleverly allows us to compare Bertha and Connie in Mellors's mind. Obviously, Bertha Coutts is not a fully developed character. She exists more as a backdrop to help us understand what Mellors is fleeing from and why he has decided to take up with Connie.

It was a schoolmaster's daughter with whom Mellors had his first sexual experience, at age 16. He was the "clever sort of young fellow from Sheffield Grammar School," and she was the "romantic sort" who pushed him into reading books. They were the most "literary-cultured couple in ten counties," Mellors explains, and he talked to her all day and worked himself up into fine intellectual excitations with her. He talked her into having sex, but she didn't want it. As with Clifford's friends at Wragby, the schoolmaster's daughter loved it when talk became the most important thing (*LCL*, 216). Mellors left her in anger and cruelty, he explains, and "took on" with a teacher, who turned out to be someone who "loved everything about love," but not sex. "Then came Bertha Coutts," he said. He had lived next door to her when he was young, and her family was "common." In fact, he liked the fact that she was common, and he wanted to be common, too. So he stopped talking "proper English," went back to "talking broad," got a job shoeing horses, and married her. She wanted him, "and made no bones about it," and that was what he wanted, "a woman who *wanted*" him (*LCL*, 217). But things did not go smoothly with Bertha, either. Very few academic commentators have paid attention to what comes next in Mellors's soliloquy, but I will, because what we find here is essential to understanding the difference between what Mellors has with Connie and what he had—and would no longer abide—with Bertha.

Mellors tells us that when he made love to Bertha, he did it very well, but that "she despised [him] a bit, for being so pleased about it." As a result, she would put him off when asked, but when he didn't want it "she'd come all lovey-dovey, and get me. And I always went. But when I had her, she'd never come-off when I did. . . . If I kept back for half an hour, she'd keep back longer. And when I'd come and really finished, then she'd start on her own account, and I had to stop inside her till she brought herself off" (*LCL*, 217). Mellors is not whining or complaining about a lack of "mutual orgasm"; rather, he is describing Coutts as masturbating against him, enjoying her power over him, as men often do with women. "I told her how I hated it. And she'd even try. She'd try to lie still and let *me* work the business.

But it was no good. She got no feeling off it, from my working. She had to work the thing herself, grind her own coffee. And it came back on her like a raving necessity, she had to let herself go, and tear, tear, tear, as if she had no sensation in her except in the top of her beak, the very outside top tip, that rubbed and tore" (*LCL*, 218).

One could argue that Mellors is simply afraid of women and their sexual responses, especially of stout Bertha, since his experiences with the other two women in his youth were quite limited. This may be true, but such a conclusion is only a guess about his character—he does not use the word *fear* in his discussions of Coutts. Robert Scholes argues that Mellors is the kind of man who fears a woman who likes "to be in control of the sexual scene," a man who also "orders the clitoris to cease and desist, orders women to be more 'feminine,' " more passive, in other words.[10] But Mellors has already explained that those women who just "lie there like nothing and let you go ahead" do not enjoy sex at all (*LCL*, 219). And he is not complaining that Bertha was being too aggressive in her enjoyment. He is saying that Bertha does not like him *as a male,* at all, the way Connie does. "I hated it. And she hated me" (*LCL*, 218; emphasis added). As Mark Spilka has pointed out, "It is Michaelis . . . and not Mellors, who fits Scholes's coding of the man who fears greater female sexuality. Mellors is by deliberate contrast a man with greater delaying powers who seeks sexual commitment with his wife, and his similar complaint against her as a woman who uses her clitoris as a weapon in the sexual fray, even as men use their penises, seems to be well taken."[11]

Of course, Mellors is by no means a perfect lover. Lawrence is not interested in giving us perfection. When Connie comments on Mellors's sexual troubles—"So when you did get a women who wanted you . . . you got a bit too much of a good thing"—and when we hear Mellors's litany about what "the mass of women" are really like, we realize that Mellors is bitter, not fearful (*LCL*, 219). He confesses to Connie: "I was really getting bitter. I thought there was not real sex left" (*LCL*, 220). Under Connie's probing remarks we finally hear what Mellors does fear, and we get an insight into his character that helps us understand his behavior in the novel.

"I knew what I wanted with a woman, and I could never say I'd
got it when I hadn't."
    "But have you got it now?"
    "Looks as if I might have."
    "Then why are you so pale and gloomy?"
    "Bellyful of remembering: and perhaps afraid of myself. . . .
And I'm very mistrustful. You'll have to expect it. It takes a lot to
make me trust anybody, inwardly. So perhaps I'm a fraud too. I
mistrust." (*LCL,* 220)

Mellors admits that he is afraid of his own feelings about
women, that he is "very mistrustful" of them, and he tells Connie that
perhaps he is "a fraud" (*LCL,* 220), a man who preaches about trust,
but when push comes to shove really does not, at bottom, trust
females. These admissions, coming as they do after his discussion of
Bertha Coutts, complicate our perception of him as Lawrence's "hero"
in this novel—they flesh out our perception of Mellors as a whole and
complex character.

To round out our view of Mellors, we briefly turn to a novel by James
Fenimore Cooper, *The Deerslayer.* We know that Lawrence read some
of Cooper's novels as a young man and loved them. And we know that
he read *The Deerslayer* in 1916 as he started to write *Women in Love,*
calling it in a letter "pure and exquisite art . . . lovely, mature and sensitive."[12] What is really surprising, however, is how closely the character of Mellors resembles Natty Bumppo, the Deerslayer in Cooper's
novel, one of America's most famous fictional characters. In
Lawrence's essay "Fenimore Cooper's Leatherstocking Novels," published in his *Studies in Classic American Literature* (1923), he describes
the Deerslayer as a "man of the woods . . . silent, simple, philosophic,
moralistic, and an unerring shot."[13] He "keeps the centre of his own
consciousness steady and unperturbed," and rather than let the women
in the novel "master him" or drag him "into a false heat of deliberate
sensuality" he remains alone to "preserve his integrity," despite his
marriage proposal in middle age ("Leatherstocking Novels," 66–67).
The Deerslayer's "stoicism" is "honest and fearless," and he "lets his

consciousness penetrate in loneliness into the new continent . . . he wrestles with the spirits of the forest and the American wild, as a hermit wrestles with God and Satan" ("Leatherstocking Novels," 67). "He is neither spiritual nor sensual. He is a moralizer, but he always tries to moralize from actual experience, not from theory" (Leatherstocking Novels," 68).

It is very tempting to see Mellors in these descriptions and we may even suggest that Cooper's Natty Bumppo embodied all the qualities Lawrence was looking to put in Mellors—especially when we read in Cooper how Bumppo affected Judith: "The freshness of his integrity, the poetry and truth of his feelings, and even the quaintness of his forms of speech all had their influence and aided in awakening an interest that she found as pure as it was sudden and deep."[14] It is very tempting indeed to say that Bumppo, the Deerslayer, was Lawrence's model for Mellors. After all, Mellors is described as having been "alone and apart from man or woman for four years," a man who "rose and took his coat again, and his gun, lowered the lamp and went out into the starry night, with the dog . . . he made his round in the wood, slowly, softly" (*LCL*, 127). But such a claim is too neat, too easy, even though we know how much Lawrence admired Cooper. In the final analysis, something very specific separates Cooper's "hero" from Lawrence's more complex character. "Hurt nothing unless you're forced to," says Bumppo in *The Deerslayer*. Yet as Lawrence points out, the Deerslayer "gets his deepest thrill of gratification, perhaps, when he puts a bullet through the heart of a beautiful buck, as it stoops to drink at the lake." And this is the "myth of the essential white America." Both men turn their back on society in order to retain their integrity and hide out in the woods. But for Bumppo, "All the other stuff, the love, the democracy, the floundering into lust, is a sort of by-play. The essential American soul is hard, isolate, stoic, and a killer" ("Leatherstocking Novels," 68). When a man like the Deerslayer "breaks from his static isolation, and makes a new move, then look out, something will be happening" ("Leatherstocking Novels," 69). When Mellors finally leaves his isolation, something is happening, but to himself and to Connie. Oliver Mellors may be, like Bumppo, "hard, isolate," and "stoic," but he is never the Western hero, never an American myth, a John Wayne, an Ernest Hemingway, or a Clint Eastwood, never an American killer. And so when Connie asks him in utter frustration, "But what do you believe in?" he answers, "I believe in being warm-hearted. I believe especially in being warm-hearted in love, in fucking with a warm heart. I believe if men could fuck with warm hearts, and the women take it warm-heartedly, everything would come all right" (*LCL*, 222). This belief is a far cry from Natty Bumppo, who says, "I would think no more of such a woman but turn my mind altogether to the forest: *that* will not deceive you (*Deerslayer*, 19).

Tommy Dukes   With his libido most likely fixed in oral stimulation, his admitted need to chatter, Tommy Dukes chews ideas and feelings to bits with his buddies at Wragby. He is the kind of man who cannot strip off his ego with his clothes, and yet the rhythmic form of his character, its honest humor, is so engaging, so truthful and witty, that we can't help but like him more than just a little bit—especially when he makes fun of himself, something no other character in the novel can do. It may be an odd thing to say, although not an exaggeration, but talk for the men at Wragby is their way of getting infantile oral satisfaction. After all, according to Lawrence, the modern woman sees the modern man as "a child with his appetites," and the woman better yield to him what he wants, "or like a child," he will "probably turn nasty" (*LCL*, 4). Later in the novel, Clifford is described as a baby in the presence of his nurse, Mrs. Bolton, and his friends Hammond, May, and Dukes do present themselves sometimes as sleeping nurslings, satiated with their own feeding on ideas.

The boys at Wragby Hall may even strike us as eternal adolescents, boy-adults who revert to being teenagers, as members of a peer group that, as Connie knew, did not "*really* want a woman" (*LCL*, 59) and who could only find reaffirmation of their egos in the need to say " 'shit!' in front of a lady" (*LCL*, 40). These men have "teenagerized" one another by separating their ideas on sex from the tenderness they are either too frightened or too bored to feel. The boredom they feel about life is really the required repression of pleasure that male social groups need to survive in their intellectual conformity. Independent couples are threats to groups, but happy, fulfilled couples are especially threatening to the Wragby men. As Hammond says, any interest in sex is really only "misplaced curiosity" (*LCL*, 31). If, therefore, one of these Wragby men were to really place his curiosity in sexual matters, instead of in the group, then his buddies would see him as a "traitor" to their group melancholia, marked as it is by boredom and sexual sadness. Lawrence himself was called a traitor to the English "war effort" and to the adolescent dream image of the romantic body in fiction and in film.

In their peer group conversations, Clifford, Hammond, Berry, May, and Dukes wait for their oral libidos to be satiated. "The arguments, the discussions were the great thing," love making for these men was just a "bit of primitive reversion" (*LCL*, 3). Group melancholia is sustained not only by the conspiracy of reinforced feelings in group membership but also by the ability to create in conversation a collective "dream screen," a surface upon which the men project their ideas about power, success, and irreversible consumption.[15] This "dream screen," the product of a collective oral melancholia in Wragby's men, helps us as readers to hear how these men project and maintain their objectivity and detachment about real sexuality and connection in order to talk about what they are actually interested in: how to use sex with a woman to bring worldly success and help feed their narcissism. Dukes says to Hammond: "men like you think you'll get through better with a woman's backing . . . sex is to you . . . a vital little dynamo between you and Julia, to bring success" (*LCL*, 32).

As Jean Baudrillard writes, we sense that these men want "sex, like power, to become an irreversible instance. . . . For we grant meaning only to what is irreversible: accumulation . . . production."[16] Of course the men at Wragby are indeed interested in *irreversible* accumulation, production, and rates of exchange, given their real interest not in sex but in property, coal mines, money, and image. They claim real sex to be a primitive *reversion* to that which cannot be "produced" at will, accumulated on demand, purchased, or seen. These men represent the exhaustion of modern sexuality, an exhaustion with themselves. Living in a consumer culture of their own design, they see women as consumable capital goods and services.

Only Tommy Dukes admits to himself and to his friends the cynicism behind their ideas on love and money, only Dukes tries to wake his peer group up from their collective "dream screen" that clouds and hides their bitterness. In chapter 4 of the novel, Dukes throws his bombs at the skull of Mammon as soon as we meet him. Hammond says that the "whole point about the sexual problem" is that there is "no point to it," it really isn't a problem, since we need not see it as more important than anything else (*LCL*, 31). On the other hand, Dukes continues, "If you began to be unsuccessful you'd begin to flirt, like Charlie, who isn't successful." If a man can't pursue the world and attain success, then he will pursue a woman to attain it. Charlie responds: "I can't see I do a woman any more harm by sleeping with her than by dancing with her . . . or even talking to her about the weather. It's just an interchange of sensations instead of ideas, so why not?" (*LCL*, 32).

Dukes finds this idea ridiculous. With sarcasm dripping from his tongue, he summarizes such a view and replaces May's word "interchange" with the key word "exchange," thereby characterizing May's view of sex for what it is: only one among all the human activities that have been reduced to equal importance for the sake of the quick buy or speedy sale. If the exchange of touch and feeling is like the exchange of words or money, then all is reduced to whether or not one got a good deal. Surface needs and personalities are preserved so that nothing will happen underneath to the essential man or woman. The purchasing power of the man and the woman is protected. Dukes has a clear view about how the culture of money has so deeply influenced our private, sexual lives. He would agree with Baudrillard here: "the sexual jurisdiction is but a fantastic extension of the commonplace ideal of private property, where everyone is assigned a certain amount of capital to manage: a psychic capital, a libidinal, sexual or unconscious capital, for which each person will have to answer individually, under the sign of his or her own liberation" (Baudrillard, 39). May says: "If you *have* the proper sort of emotion or sympathy with a woman, you *ought* to sleep with her" (*LCL*, 33).

But of course Dukes has all along objected to what May and Clifford call "proper" emotion. What is this proper emotion for a woman? It is when sex is put in its "proper" place for these men: on an open market manufactured to appear user friendly. It becomes something that does not disturb even the surface of their lives, their "home," money, success mongering, or flirtations. The proper sexual emotion for a woman is a "sort of communication like speech" (*LCL*, 34–35), a polite exchange of words. Tommy Dukes admits: "Let any woman start a sex conversation with me, and it's natural for me to go to bed with her to finish it" (*LCL*, 35). Does the "it" refer to the sex or to the talk? That's the wrong question to ask in an overheated market. Sex=Talk. Talk=Sex. Both are compressed in the social good deal that is struck between melancholic partners. Talk *is* sex for these men because it is speedy, efficient, a technological buy and sell. Of course, Dukes further admits with bitter good humor that no woman "makes any particular start with" him, and that's because he can't play the market anymore, he can't play the game. Yet Lawrence's powerful and disturbing point is made through Duke's strategic use of that "it": that when one "uncovers in the body's secret places an 'unbound' libidinal energy opposed to the 'bound' energy" of the surface power game of talk, that checkmate of flirtation in getting more sex-cash, "when one uncovers in desire the truth of the body's phantasms and drives, one is still only disintering the psychic metaphor of capital" (Baudrillard, 39). Even in our deepest love-desire, Lawrence says, purchasing power has its effect. Yet Lawrence believes that the novel can reveal the most secret places of life, and he hopes that the "tide of sensitive awareness" we get from *Lady Chatterley's Lover* will be able to clean and freshen those places, perhaps even "lead into new places" (*LCL*, 106), places in us somehow free from the bitter purchasing of power with sex-cash. Can this novel perform such a task for a reader? Is it true that "there can be no thorough 'sex in the head' experience of this novel," because the book is "too direct and effective to permit that?" And is it true that this novel "is bound to have resonance within the body"[17] itself, despite the disinterment of what Baudrillard calls our deepest "psychic metaphor of capital?" Lawrence's clean and freshened secret place in us, our essential sex, "our center of gravity," has been, today, "displaced towards a libidinal economy concerned with only . . . a desire dedicated to drives, or to a machine-like functioning," as Baudrillard writes.

"You have a sex, and you must put it to good use."
> "You have an unconscious, and you must let the id speak."
> "You have a body, and you must derive pleasure from it."
> "You have a libido, and you must expend it," etc.

This pressure towards liquidity, flux and the accelerated articulation of the sexual, psychic and physical body is an exact replica of that which regulates exchange value: capital must circulate, there must no longer be any fixed point, investments must be ceaselessly renewed, value must radiate without respite—this is the form of value's present realization, and sexuality, the sexual *model,* is simply its mode of appearance at the level of the body.

As a model sex takes the form of an *individual* enterprise based on natural energy: to each his desire and may the best man prevail (in matters of pleasure). (Baudrillard, 38)

Dukes would agree with such a bleak summary of our modern emotions. For as Lawrence's creation, he is a summary of only one man's attempt and failure at experiencing or achieving the "cleansing and freshening" of his "passional secret places of life" (*LCL,* 106), and he makes no bones about it in chapter 6. Connie asks Dukes how men could love women without talking to them. "Well," Tommy says, "I don't know. What's the use of my generalizing? I only know my own case. I like women, but I don't desire them. . . . Who's going to force me into loving, or pretending to love them, working up the sex game?" (*LCL,* 58). Connie feels sorry for him, but Dukes is not in the least interested in feeling sorry for himself. He is simply not interested, nor perhaps has he ever been interested, in "parading the sex thing." Damn the "artificial sex-compulsion!" he says. We can't take Dukes as a "general example" of men because he is "just a special case," only one member of the Wragby group (*LCL,* 58). Nor can we generalize and say that all readers *will* get from this book what Lawrence wants them to get, that they *will* feel the novel in their bodies. For each of us is a "special case," a someone who may or may not be able to change his or her "machine-like functioning," a someone who may or may not understand his or her capital drives, a someone who may or may not feel the need or find a way to cleanse the secret place. We can only hope, the way the novel so beautifully hopes, the way Connie and Mellors hope to break away from the cash gang.

Yet if we do find ourselves wanting to get what Lawrence desires that we do from this novel, then we also know that there will be a knock-down-drag-out fight to get it. For it will be a personal fight against spite, politics, and the love games triggered by the modern consumerism of our *sexyeconomics,* that system of exchange wherein all things as well as love are characterized by the cold come-on. And since everything is saturated with undifferentiated sex, the "fun" in the collective game of being and feeling *sexploited* is not to succumb to love (for that would end the game) but to continue within a pattern that provides a mental "win." It is no longer a matter of connection, but one of self-identification. The endgame of the verbal contest is not passion, but recognition, self-reinforcement, neutered enjoyment. That is why Tommy Dukes says that "the tie that binds *us* just now is mental friction," that our mental lives flourish with their "roots in spite . . . the sheer joy in pulling somebody else to bits" in the verbal contest (*LCL,* 36). In modern love, friction is fun, for it anchors itself in the absorption that "gets its" man or woman by denying love depth. The deep essential nature of love is neutered by the flashing question from the advertised body: "Do you mind my fixated egoism?" The cold come-on in the melancholic sex game is not the offer of pleasure but the quest for purchase. Modern love is brain love, ad-tickled by the porn image to choose from a soft array of boxed goods. Your "basic bodily attitude," says Wilhelm Reich, "is that of *holding back* and of *spite;* because panic strikes you when the primordial movement of LOVE and GIVING stirs in you. This is why you are *afraid of giving.* Your taking, basically, has only *one* meaning: You are forced continually to gorge yourself with money, with happiness, with knowledge, because you feel yourself to be empty, starved, unhappy, not genuinely knowing nor desirous of knowledge. For the same reason you keep running away from the truth, Little Man: it might release the love reflex in you. . . . And that you do not want . . . You only want to be a consumer and a patriot."[17]

Dukes would agree here—even though he admits that he can't "vibrate in unison with a woman" (40). That's why he preaches to the little men of Wragby: "Real knowledge comes out of the whole corpus of the consciousness; out of your belly and your penis as much as out of your brain and mind" (*LCL*, 37). But what about the social web? Doesn't the study of politics show that we are trapped? Caught in the webbing of political engineering and hate? Unable to get "real knowledge?" The young man Berry turns Dukes's preaching to politics when he implies all the above questions with his "But what do you think of Bolshevism?" (*LCL*, 38). Dukes's response is quick: "One has to be human, and have a heart and a penis if one is going to escape" being a Bolshevist or a good bourgeois property-man, or if one is going to fight the collective "dream screen" (*LCL*, 39). For Dukes believes, as does Lawrence, that "*our deepest feelings we force according to certain ideas,*" instead of basing our ideas about how we should live upon our feelings. Yet when Berry asks Dukes if he believes in love, Dukes responds in the only way *he* can—"I don't believe in it at all" (*LCL*, 39). Once again, that "it."

Is Lawrence making his point that Dukes is incapable of learning what Mellors learns at the end of the novel? That having the courage of one's own tenderness for a woman is the only way to fight your way free from the tough, fibrous webbing of the utopian social collective? Or does that "it" refer to only the "joint-property, make-a-success-of-it" brand of modern brain love, that capital drive found deep, even in our most secret places? (*LCL*, 39). We admire Dukes's courage at admitting that he does not have what Lawrence will give to Mellors— the rebel's "good heart," "chirpy penis," and "lively intelligence" (*LCL*, 40)—and we understand why he says that he is "only a 'mental-lifer' " (*LCL*, 40). That is the only thing he can be. Only when Connie finally remarks that there really *are* nice women in the world, however, do we finally understand what we have suspected all along: that Wragby men deeply resented Connie saying anything at all, resented her even being there in the room, resented, in other words, the female. They all "hated" the fact that she had even listened to *the talks*—even Tommy Dukes (*LCL*, 40). They have run from woman to take refuge against her in the collective melancholic comfort of the group: that modern group, so user friendly to our *sexyeconomics,* wherein even

Tommy, concludes Connie, "ended," like a nursling, in "himself"
(*LCL*, 66).

The Aesthetics of Woundings

As we said earlier, all of the characters in *Lady Chatterley's Lover* suffer from a modern *wounding* of one kind or another. When Connie asks Tommy Dukes why men and women do not really like each other, Dukes can respond only in *his* own way, only in a way that satisfies him, as he repairs the psychic wounds he feels from the Great War and from the death of meaning behind the old, great words. "I like women and talk to them," Dukes says, "and therefore I don't love them and desire them. The two things don't happen at the same time in me" (*LCL*, 57).

> "I think they ought to" [Connie said].
> "All right. The fact that things ought to be something else than what they are is not my department."
> Connie considered this—"It isn't true," she said. "Men can love women and talk to them. I don't see how they can love them *without* talking, and being friendly and intimate. How can they?"
> "Well," he said, "I don't know. What's the use of my generalizing? I only know my own case. I like women, but I don't desire them." (*LCL*, 57–58)

Dukes has found his own way of healing, as Clifford has, and Mellors. To assuage her wounds, Connie walks into the forest because she likes the "inwardness" of the woods, the power of its silence, and the strong security in the aloneness of the trees—things she felt in opposition to the people at Wragby. In chapter 6, when she saw Mellors bathing, she felt more than just rebellion or strength in the wood, she received the sight as a "hit" in the middle of her body, a shock to her womb. Seeing Mellors as a "creature purely alone" overwhelms her. It was neither beauty nor a popular romantic attachment to nature that held her vision but Mellors as a single life, a "solitary nudity" (*LCL,* 68). Lawrence is telling us in this scene to beware of romance, to beware of people who "love nature, or flowers, or dogs, or babies, or pure adventure. It means they are getting into a love-swing where everything is easy and nothing opposes their egoism."[18] Connie is not falling into a love-swing here; on the contrary, Mellors's solitary life opposes Connie's egoism, opposes it enough to make her ridicule Mellors "with her mind" (*LCL,* 68). What she is experiencing here, what she will fight at first, is not romantic love as we know it today in our movies, Broadway plays, popular novels, and television, but something that she will dislike, something that will get under the ideal image of herself in love.

James Joyce and Virginia Woolf, Lawrence's famous contemporaries, also sought solutions in their fiction to the wound of history and to what they saw as the failure of modern love.[19] To relieve the tension of living under the yoke of history, however, Joyce wrote *Ulysses* (1922) and illustrated how life could be fused with art, while Woolf intended *Between the Acts* (1941) to be her final statement on how present experience could be fused with literary and historical analogies. Both authors sought refuge from sexual turmoil, too, and their fictional technique of *monologue intérieur* explained and relieved their alienation, their nightmares about history and sex. They both wanted to portray the tragedy of modern life, and they do, superbly, by giving us the clash between their ideals and twentieth-century reality. And they tell us that life is tragic—indeed, it can be and certainly remains so in their fiction. They also wanted to portray the sterility of sexual relationships between modern men and women. They do this superbly, too, as does D. H. Lawrence in the last sections of *The Rainbow* (1915) and in *Women in Love* (1920). But *Lady Chatterley's Lover,* Lawrence does not abstract the nightmare of history and sex; instead, he exposes and then confronts our ideals about history and sex and, in the process, and despite his own ideals, suggests possible answers to the nightmare.

Lawrence does not see, as does Joyce, that men are always condemned to be at the mercy of the "Willful Woman," nor does he see, as does Woolf, that men and women are trapped and caged forever in some cruel, evolutionary cycle of sex-hate. Lawrence differs from both authors because for him the relationship between men and women is the only "great relationship," the "quick and central clue to life, not the man nor the woman, nor the children that result from the relationship."[20]

Joyce sees modern man as a humorous cuckold, who sleeps upside down with his female archetype—as does Bloom with "Molly," Joyce's "symbol" for what is important in life: a female principle. The final chapter of *Ulysses*, "Penelope," seen so frequently as affirming "Life" and the positive images of Molly, is actually the best example for seeing Molly as Joyce's personal archetype of the Irish Woman of Will. "I knew I could always get round him and I gave him all the pleasures I could leading him on till he asked me to say yes . . . "[21] Taking advantage of Bloom's psychology by stimulating his fetishes, Molly knows she can get what she wants from him: money. Bloom's request for eggs in bed is hardly the announcement for a return of liveliness in Bloom, hardly the sign that Bloom has become more virile, despite, I am sure, Joyce's awareness that the word *eggs* in Spanish (*huevos*) can be used either as a slang term for human male testicles or for implying manliness. Here is Molly's response to the request: "Ill throw him up his eggs . . . I suppose hed like my nice cream too I know what Ill do Ill go about rather gay . . . Ill put on my best shift and drawers let him have a good eyeful out of that to make his micky stand for him . . . unless I made him stand there and put him into me Ive a mind to tell him every scrap and make him do it in front of me" (*Ulysses*, 780). The supposed solution of "Penelope" to the sadism of Irish history, to the "nightmare of history" in general, is hardly provided here. So may readers have wanted Molly to be that solution. But she is not. It is the sadomasochistic relationship between Molly and Bloom that keeps this chapter from becoming any sort of affirmation of positive life. If anything, the chapter is a courageous and humorous description of Joyce's own sexual problems or the sexual problems of the surrounding culture.

Woolf's final statement on the relationship between men and women is no less pessimistic. It concentrates on the repetitive, inflexible biological role of the male, who must inevitably, according to obvious natural law, fight with and embrace the female. At the end of *Between the Acts*, after Lucy puts down her book *Outline of History*, where she has been looking at pictures of prehistoric birds, and after Giles crumples up the newspaper and turns out the light, we read: "Alone, enmity was barred; also love. Before they slept, they must fight; after they had fought, they would embrace. From that embrace another life might be born. But first they must fight, as the dog fox fights with the vixen, in the heart of darkness, in the fields of night" (*Acts*, 219). True enough, we might say, but the whole of Woolf's last novel tells us that art and love are dead and that the characters in such a dead world, a world on the verge of war, cannot regain feelings of life. The very first paragraph of *Lady Chatterley's Lover* takes the opposing view: love is alive, and people can regain feelings of life, no matter how many wars.

What D. H. Lawrence had said all along, however, was that historical progress in that flabby sense of spiritual advancement had never been real; and love, he said, conscious, Western, *romantic* love, was just as dead. Both ideas breed a compulsory disappointment in seeing their ideals collapse at the hands of physical passion. Lawrence's most successful way of breaking new ground for the novel and of breaking away from Joyce and Woolf was to characterize the relationships between men and women with feelings that were different from those found in Joyce and Woolf. Scenes like the one in which Connie sees Mellors as he is washing behind his cabin are not " 'set pieces,' epiphanies as they are in Joyce" (like Stephen's epiphany of the bathing girl in chapter 4 of *A Portrait of the Artist as a Young Man*), or like Woolf's "tableaux" in *Between the Acts*. "They are not the final *Word*, . . . they are but feelings in the developing relationship between the man and the woman" (Burns 1968, 204).

Lawrence is not talking about romantic love in such scenes. And he had no interest in giving us the archetype of the male or female (i.e., "dog fox" and "vixen"), nor is he interested in symbolic presentations of the sexes. What he wanted to capture by "getting beneath personalities and ego" and "going behind or through our idealized self-images" was not an abstract symbol or cosmic force, but the "essential man and the essential woman, i.e., what the man feels for the woman and woman for the man—apart from or in spite of their mental ideas and ideals and self-images (Burns 1968, 206). This is what makes Lawrence's novels so different from Joyce's or Woolf's, and this is what makes reading *Lady Chatterley's Lover* such a vivid aesthetic experience, a sometimes wounding aesthetic experience.

In his essay "The Novel and the Feelings," Lawrence tried to tell us why reading novels is so important. He said first that our modern society ignores the health of our feelings. "Our civilization, as far as our own souls go has been a destructive process, up to now." He said that our souls are burnt landscapes where we must "sow wild seeds" again. "We have to cultivate our feelings" ("Feelings," 758). Then he said we must return to taking care of our deepest inner meanings. How do we do this? As we read *Lady Chatterley's Lover*, Lawrence wants us to pay attention to how we react to the ideas in his novel, to how his novel begins to "sow wild seeds" in us, so that we find ourselves stepping into the dark of unknown feelings and really new ideas. And even if we can't "hear the cries far down in our own forests of dark veins," or feel the wild seeds of new ideas growing, we can "look in the real novels, and there listen-in" ("Feelings," 759–60). By helping us to listen to these cries, Lawrence rips a hole in the veil of aesthetic distance and then shoves us through it. He rips "the old veil of a vision across" so that readers can find out what their hearts really believe in, what their hearts really want (*Unconscious*, 57). How does he do it?

Traditional concepts of aesthetic distance stress that readers maintain cool objectivity to understand the work of art, that they keep their lives out of their responses to the material. This is an impossible thing to do with *Lady Chatterley's Lover*, and Lawrence knew that. He knew that by devoting this novel to the struggle involved in sexual fulfillment he would be ripping a hole in the veil of our aesthetic distance and closing the distance between us and his novel. He was the kind of artist who wasn't afraid to tell his publishers and his friends that if they wanted to feel safe, then they should read somebody else. Lawrence kicks our chins in this novel, wakes us up, wounds us, prods us to ask questions about our own lives, disturbs our sleep, makes us feel nervous as we read about the struggle for love between Connie and Mellors. This novel shoves us through the hole in the veil because Lawrence gets under our idealized self-images and digs out the essential male and female in us, whatever they might be, so that we find out what our hearts want or do not want. The intensity of our reading experience will depend on how close we get to the novel, how honestly we connect our lives up to the lives in the story. The more intensely the conflicts in this novel touch us, the bigger the hole in the veil of aesthetic distance, and thus the harder it is to stay cool as we walk through the Lawrentian tear to greet the novel on its own terms. The novel especially deflates the idea of aesthetic distance *in the classroom* because there good discussions are usually too visceral, and because the feelings we may have about sexual fulfillment and those feelings Connie and Mellors may have about it are either coincidental or in deep conflict with one another. And if they are in deep conflict, we will often keep our wounded feelings distant from the story because the attack mounted by the novel is an attack on our ideals about love. The bomb this novel throws at us is the bomb Lawrence lobs at our belief in ideal love.[22]

There is a wall of objectivity we need to read a work like *Ulysses,* but it crumbles when we read a Lawrence novel, because Lawrence could not write a novel to be something we would sit back and admire. By stating that a book should be a bandit or a rebel, Lawrence takes the novel far beyond the aesthetics of Joyce and Woolf. This is not to say that Lawrence was not moved to despair over war, as were Joyce and Woolf, or that he remained aloof from theories of history. He was greatly disturbed by both. Indeed, his early story "England, My England" (1915), often called Lawrence's "English Elegy,"[23] and his chapter "The Nightmare" from his novel *Kangaroo* (1923) beautifully testify to his struggles with the reality of war. And as far as Lawrence's struggle with the death of old, rural England is concerned, *The Rainbow* (1915) is not only the novel that deals with that, but it is also a book that explores the very real and deeper historical effects industrialization brought to our emotional and sexual lives.

REFUGE

As we have seen, Lawrence establishes in the first seven chapters of this novel a sharp contrast between Wragby and the wood. But he is also describing the gradual and impending changes in Connie Chatterley.

Standing naked in front of her bedroom mirror in chapter 7, Connie examines her body. She sees it growing dull, shapeless, losing the gleam it had "in the days of her German boy, who really loved her physically" but who is now dead in the war (*LCL,* 72). Growing rebellion smolders deep inside her because a physical sense of injustice begins to burn there too, an anger at Clifford and all the men of Wragby. The politics, the chatter, the money grubbing, the "mental life!" she thinks. "Suddenly she hated it with a rushing fury, the swindle!" (*LCL,* 73). Clifford never really was nor could be warm, as Connie's father could be "with the warmth of a man who did himself well, and intended to, but who still could comfort a woman with a bit of his masculine glow" (*LCL,* 74). In fact, Connie thinks, our whole modern race is hard and separate, and warmth for us is just "bad taste" (*LCL,* 74). A conversation about the future of civilization among Wragby regulars Lady Bennerley, Tommy Dukes, Harry Winterslow, and Jack and Olive Strangeways substantiates Connie's theory here. Olive proclaims that true freedom will come when women are no longer "dragged down" by their *functions,* and Jack sees governments releasing ether into the air so that we can all be permanently amused. Lady Bennerley says that if "civilization is any good, it has to help us forget our bodies" (*LCL,* 77). Of course, Dukes denies all of this and announces that the only bridge to the future will be the phallus. Connie is bored by all the talk, and since Mrs. Bolton is now caring for her husband, she feels ready to be released. We now sense, finally, she will enter a new phase in which her life will change.

The remaining chapters of *Lady Chatterley's Lover* will show us Connie and Mellors fleeing their respective worlds by freeing themselves emotionally from the demands of convention. They will do so not as cardboard cutouts of "their class" but as individuals: Connie from Wragby and modern love, and Mellors from Tevershall and money grubbing. Both seek refuge in the wood, that "country in between" so important to Lawrence where there is what he called in his "Autobiographical Fragment" that "lonely sort of fierceness and beauty" (817).

5

Bomb

This is where I throw a straight bomb at the skull of idealistic Mammon.

—D. H. Lawrence on *Lady Chatterley's Lover*, 1928

THE KEY

Chapter 8 opens with Connie once again escaping to the woods. She sits down "with her back to a young pine tree," feeling still and alone, and gets into the "current of her own proper destiny" (*LCL*, 89–90). We learn too that because Mellors's own proper destiny is solitude, he resents Connie's presence. "Especially he did not want to come into contact with a woman again. He feared it, for he had a big wound from old contacts. He felt if he could not be alone, and if he could not be left alone, he would die. His recoil away from the outer world was complete; his last refuge was this wood; to hide himself there!" (*LCL*, 92).

What attracts Connie to Mellors is also what repels her. For, as we have seen, she sees in him a solitary and intent "animal" that works alone, "the stillness and the timeless sort of patience, in a man impatient and passionate," and this, Lawrence makes a point of telling us, touches her womb. Yet she also feels the inherent resistance of a man like this to her will. Mellors dreads Connie's "female will," her "modern female insistency," and her "upper-class impudence" at getting her own way (*LCL,* 93). Connie senses his resistance to her. Their fight over her request for a key to his hut ends with both of them feeling angry over each other's "self-will." "She had wakened the sleeping dogs of old voracious anger in him, anger against the self-willed female. . . . And she was angry against the self-willed male. A servant too! She walked sullenly home" (*LCL,* 94). This fight, this confrontation between male and female individualities and self-willed behavior, characterizes Lawrence's definition of love between the sexes. *Lady Chatterley's Lover* is a novel that explores this conflict, and shows us that often the conflict is resolved, and often it is not. What is important for Lawrence is not the happy endings but the see-saw battle of wills, that fight toward regeneration for the sexes, a battle that repeats itself often for connection.

When Connie tries to explain to Mellors that she wanted the key to his hut so that she could have a place to be alone, the fight starts:

> "I won't trouble you. But I don't think I should have minded at all sitting and seeing you look after the birds. . . . But since you think it interferes with you, I won't disturb you, don't be afraid. You are Sir Clifford's keeper, not mine. . . ."
>
> "Nay, your Ladyship. It's your Ladyship's own 'ut. It's as your Ladyship likes an' pleases, every time. . . . On'y as 'appen yo'd like the place ter yersen, when yer did come, an' not me messin' abaht."
>
> ". . . Why should I take any notice of you and your being here or not? Why is it important?"
>
> He looked at her, all his face glimmering with wicked laughter.
>
> "It's not, your Ladyship. Not in the very least," he said.
>
> "Well, why then?" she asked.

"Shall I get your Ladyship another key then?"
"No, thank you! I don't want it." (*LCL,* 99–100)

Connie leaves, feeling insulted and angry with his need for solitude. Mellors enjoys the argument a little bit, with his "wicked laugh-
ter," giving it just once to the upper crust. Yet Connie learns in
chapter 9 that she prefers Mellors's stubborn solitude to Clifford's
world, even though their fight over the key illustrates the differences
between their class standing. Clifford's maleness is no longer directed
toward a regenerative fight for love but toward capturing the bitch-
goddess of success and money "by brute means of industrial production." This is what gets "his pecker up" (*LCL,* 112). But this is not
what gets Mellors's pecker up. Clifford studies modern methods of
coal mining and "management" and feels a surge of power flow
through him, power over men, money, and the world. What begins to
surge through Mellors in chapter 10 is not power, but compassion for
Connie.

MIDPOINT SUMMARY

Chapter 10 is almost exactly halfway through the novel, and in many
ways it functions as a brief summary of Lawrence's main ideas in the
book. Perhaps we can summarize his ideas in the following way.

1. *Nature is regenerative for human beings.*
Lawrence is famous for his magnificent descriptions of the natural
world. In his nature essays, like "Whistling of Birds," in his poetry, like
Birds, Beasts, and Flowers, in travel books, like *Twilight in Italy,* and in
his letters, we witness a sensitive, acute, and brilliant perception at
work as it describes the magic of plant and animal life. He was no less
brilliant in his use of natural imagery for his fiction. Whether it be in
the stunning opening pages of his novel *The Rainbow* or in the poems
and stories he wrote in New Mexico, all of his writings testify to a
deep love for the natural world around him. He believed nature to be
a force for renewal as well as for destruction, a cleansing force that

often helped his characters find what their hearts really wanted and believed in.

Connie walks into the woods to see Mellors in chapter 10 and "all the trees [are] making a silent effort to open their buds . . . she could almost feel it in her own body, the huge heave of the sap in the massive trees, upwards, up, up to the bud-tips, there to push into little flamey oak leaves, bronze as blood" (*LCL,* 129). Nature's renewal helps Connie to feel renewal because Lawrence believes that human beings need the qualities of natural growth around them to remind them of what is really important in life. Connie is conscious of an energy from the trees crossing over into her being as she struggles for renewal.

Opposed to Wragby and the industrial landscape, the wood, through Lawrence's vibrant language, looms wise in its mysterious serenity as a retreat from a world where power and social engineering are the prime values. Disgusted with Clifford and his modern, industrial, and financial world, Connie turns once and for all to Mellors. She waits for him to return to the hut.

> The wood was silent, still and secret in the evening drizzle of rain, full of the mystery of eggs and half-open buds, half-unsheathed flowers. . . . How still everything was! The fine rain blew very softly, filmily, but the wind made no noise. Nothing made any sound. The trees stood like powerful beings, dim, twilit, silent and alive. How alive everything was! (*LCL,* 130)

2. *Love is a struggle characterized by the natural fear of the differences between male and female.*

Chapter 10 is dominated by what Connie and Mellors are learning about the renewal of their feelings as they struggle to live in Lawrence's "country in between." Feeling "broken open" again and knowing that he has lost his privacy, Mellors knows that the safety and privacy of the wood is an illusion: the modern world "allows no hermits" (*LCL,* 125–26). He does not blame Connie for his reluctance to feel again, but he does blame the "insentient iron world and the Mammon of mechanized greed" (*LCL,* 127). For such a world will complicate and destroy what he could have with such a woman. He was "consciously afraid of society, which he knew by instinct to be a malevolent, partly-insane beast" (*LCL*, 127).

Connie admits that her womb *almost* opened to him because he was kind "to the female in her, which no man had ever been" (*LCL*, 129). Yet she fears losing herself to him and resolves to regain her will, to regain the upper hand. But when they meet after Connie returns from the Marehay Farm after visiting Mrs. Flint and her baby, she loses her will as Mellors leads her through a wall of "prickly trees" (*LCL*, 141). They make love, and Connie is "unconscious of the wild little cries" she utters (*LCL*, 142). She feels alive, vulnerable, filled with love for a man she neither expected nor wanted. She is carried away by the feelings in her womb at having a child by him, yet she resents such feelings, too. For she does not want to "lose herself" at all, to be "a slave" to a man, a mere "phallus bearer." She does not want Mellors to "intrude" upon her, she does not want to give up her "hard bright female power" (*LCL*, 144).

Mellors's feelings for Connie are equally powerful and ambivalent. That night he sleeps little, and, wandering out into the forest, thinks that if he did get entangled with this woman it would bring nothing but bitterness and trouble. Since he refuses to care about money and hates the world of greed in the cities and factories, what will he do? How will he make a life for them both? He wanders up to Wragby Hall and stands there, looking at the estate.

> With a sudden snap the bleeding desire that had drawn him after her broke. He had broken it, because it must be so. There must be a coming together on both sides. And if she wasn't coming to him, he wouldn't track her down. He mustn't. He must go away, till she came.
>
> He turned slowly, ponderingly, accepting again the isolation. He knew it was better so. She must come to him: it was no use his trailing after her. No use! (*LCL*, 155)

This fluctuation in feeling characterizes the love between these people throughout the novel. It is the fluctuation of feeling in individuals who need to remain solitary, who need to remain independent in their maleness and femaleness and yet who feel drawn to their union. It is a fluctuation in the kind of love that Lawrence wishes to define in this novel, a love that starts out unconscious in its desire (as it does when Mellors finds himself touching Connie "with a blind stroking motion" [*LCL*, 123]), but then finishes with conscious resolves: "She watched his face, and the passion for him moved in her bowels. She resisted it as far as she could, for it was the loss of herself to herself" (*LCL*, 143).

So, there is this togetherness about them. Can we call it love? "You can't call it love," Lawrence says. "It would be too ridiculous. . . . As far as I can see, it is desire."

> And the desire has a fluctuating intensity, but it is always there. . . .
> It would be false to call it love, because love complicates the ego.
> The ego is always concerned in love. But in the frail, subtle desirousness of the true male, towards everything female, and the equally frail, indescribable desirability of every female for every male, lies the real clue to the equating, or the *relating*, of things which otherwise are incommensurable.
>
> And this, this desire, is the reality which is inside love.
> ("Little Boy," 451–52)

3. *Both men and women must fight to preserve real desire.*
Solitary, mistrustful of women, full of hate for the world's "Mammon of mechanized greed" (*LCL*, 127), and in dread at the thought of exposing himself to "that outside Thing that sparkled viciously in the electric lights," Mellors still knew that he was driven by real desire for Connie, a desire that would lead them both into a social mess. Yet it is clear that Mellors would fight for it, "if only there were other men to be with, to fight that sparkling electric Thing outside there" (the city, with its pursuit of money and status, and English society in general, with its class divisions). He would fight "to preserve the tenderness of life, the tenderness of women, and the natural riches of desire" (*LCL*, 127–28). But there are no other men to fight with. Mellors must go it alone. He will fight his own fear of Connie, and his fear of real desire. "So if I've got to be broken open again," he says, "I have" (*LCL*, 125).

Alienated, mistrustful of Mellors, full of hate for Clifford's world, and in dread of giving herself completely to a man, Connie nevertheless knew that she was driven by real desire for the gamekeeper. She knew well enough the social mess it would be for her. Yet it is clear in this chapter that despite her misgivings about Mellors, she is ready to fight alone for her desires even before Mellors realizes that he must do the same. She can think to herself—"What sort of a man was he, really? Did he really like her? Not much, she felt" (*LCL*, 128)—and then turn around and defend to Mellors's face her desire for him, despite the consequences.

> ". . . I don't care what happens to me."
>
> "Ay, you think that! But you'll care! You'll have to care, everybody has. You've got to remember your ladyship is carrying on with a gamekeeper. It's not as if I was a gentleman. Yes, you'd care. You'd care.
>
> "I shouldn't. What do I care about my ladyship. I hate it really." (*LCL*, 132)

Their fight to preserve their love will continue to the end of the novel, but with no guarantees to the reader of a happy ending. And it will be Connie who fights the most, announcing her intentions to have Mellors's child to Clifford and her sister, Hilda, and fighting with Mellors to convince him of the rightness of their desires.

4. *The beauty of touch is deeper than the beauty of wisdom.*
Though it is only the second time they make love, it is clear in chapter 10 that a deep and mysterious touch between Connie and Mellors has taken place. Connie is still self-conscious, yet she wonders why it was so rapturous for Mellors to touch her belly and thighs. "She did not understand the beauty he found in her, through touch upon her living secret body . . . [the] warm, live beauty of contact, so much deeper than the beauty of wisdom" (*LCL*, 133). Connie feels something that is deeper than the act of intellectual "understanding," and that's why far "down in her" she begins to feel "a new stirring, a new nakedness emerging." And she fears it. "Half she wished he would not caress her so" (*LCL*, 133).

Mrs. Bolton defines the effect of this touch, as she wonders who Lady Chatterley's lover could be and remembers her dead husband, Ted, killed in the coal mines: "when she thought of him, the old, old grudge against the world rose up, but especially against the masters, that they had killed him. They had not really killed him. Yet, to her, emotionally, they had. And somewhere deep in herself, because of it, she was a nihilist, and really anarchic" (*LCL,* 149). Connie sees in her face the same anarchic rebellion she sees in Mellors.

> "And it took me a thousand shocks before I knew he wouldn't come back, it took me years."
> "The touch of him," said Connie.
> "That's it my Lady! the touch of him! I've never got over it to this day, and never shall. And if there's a heaven above, he'll be there, and will lie up against me so I can sleep."
> Connie glanced at the handsome, brooding face in fear. Another passionate one out of Tevershall! (*LCL,* 176)

Of course how Mellors touches Connie and what he says about female sexual response has been discussed for years by critics who focus on Lawrence's personal feelings for women: from Simone de Beauvoir's *The Second Sex* (1953), which critiqued Lawrence as only a writer of guidebooks for proper female behavior, to Kate Millet, who said in *Sexual Politics* (1970) that Mellors wants to kill women who get clitoral pleasure, to Peter Balbert in *D. H. Lawrence and the Phallic Imagination* (1989), who supported Lawrence because he saw Mellors as a man who recognizes the fundamental otherness of women, to Kingsley Widmer's compromise position in *Defiant Desire* (1992), that although Lawrence gives us only formulas for proper heterosexual behavior, he remains the prophet of passionate rebellion against a sense-deadening world. Strong merits as well as logical weaknesses can be found in these arguments. But one fact remains: these feelings about touch that Bolton and Connie discuss are dramatized in chapters 14 and 18 in some of the most remarkable conversations ever penned for an English-language novel, as Connie and Mellors talk and fight for the touch that is deeper than philosophy.

BOMBS

Since Lawrence's ideas on sex and love are central to *Lady Chatterley's Lover,* and since they remain his most controversial ideas, we will look a little more closely at the message in the second item in the preceding list.

Chapter 12 beautifully illustrates the struggle between men and women in love when desire does and does not flow, or when they find power over their bodies more rewarding than letting go of their emotions. After Connie and Mellors argue over whether Connie had been using him to get pregnant, they try to make love. This time, however, Connie stiffens in resistance to the act.

> [S]omething in her spirit stiffened in resistance: stiffened from the terribly physical intimacy, and from the peculiar haste of his possession. And this time the sharp ecstasy of her own passion did not overcome her; she lay with her hands inert on his striving body, and do what she might, her spirit seemed to look on from the top of her head, and the butting of his haunches seemed ridiculous to her, and the sort of anxiety of his penis to come to its little evacuating crisis seemed farcical. Yes, this was love, this ridiculous bouncing of the buttocks . . .
>
> Cold and derisive her queer female mind stood apart, and though she lay perfectly still, her impulse was to heave her loins, and throw the man out, escape his ugly grip. (*LCL,* 184–85)

This is a powerful description of "cerebral consciousness," of mind over matter. Yet it is also an honest admission that in love making, human beings may find themselves driven to maintain their solitude and self-will. Connie and Mellors are both tormented by a "double consciousness" (*LCL,* 185), a struggle between the cerebral self and the phallic self. Carol Dix, in *D. H. Lawrence and Women* (1980), points out that the first thing to accept about the phrase "phallic consciousness" is that "in taking the word 'phallic' too literally, as meaning just male sexuality, you run the danger of misinterpreting his full intent. Lawrence did see the phallus as the vital connection between the life force of man and that of woman. But then, like any two parts, the one is rendered inactive and inert without the other. The 'phallic consciousness' is the term used to mean an awareness, an opening up to, the forces of deep, instinctual sexuality, not a holding back to the mental form of sex he saw in western society, that he calls 'sex in the head.' "[1]

After Connie confesses that she "can't love," Mellors responds that they will "ta'e th' rough wi'th' smooth" (LCL, 185). Then, even though she hates his dialect and finds him a "half-bred fellow," she still asks him to hold her, for it was "from herself she wanted to be saved, from her own inward anger and resistance" (LCL, 186). He holds her, and her "self," her cerebral self, melts away. When they make love this time, both Connie and Mellors submerge into phallic consciousness. She becomes "infinitely desirable" and tender to him, and she "went all open to him." For her it "came with a strange slow thrust of peace, the dark thrust of peace and a ponderous, primordial tenderness, such as made the world in the beginning . . . the quick of all her plasm was touched" (LCL, 186–87). And for him, he was "still with her, in an unfathomable silence along with her. And of this, they would never speak" (LCL, 188). In sharp contrast to the opening chapters of this novel, with all the "talk" about love, is this "unfathomable silence" between Connie and Mellors. It is a silence and a stillness about which they will never speak because it comes from so complete an individual experience that each has had with the other in the darkness of phallic consciousness. It is so individual that neither of them can talk about it, and yet it remains regenerative. Both of them have fought their way out of self-consciousness only to fight each other out of it, too. Sex is "a polarization of the individual blood in man towards the individual blood in woman" (Unconscious, 212).

Coupled with Lawrence's important ideas on phallic consciousness is an equally important Lawrentian idea: that we are living in an age in which the human being's instinctive trust in life has collapsed. In his essay "Return to Bestwood," Lawrence explains how things had changed in his native village since his boyhood. He remembered the men of his village from his childhood as lively, noisy, with "strong underworld voices such as I have never heard in any other men," men who had a "strange power of life in them, something wild and urgent" ("Bestwood," 263). They had an eagerness for life.

But since the war, Lawrence believed, his generation had gone "silent." They "go to the welfare clubs and drink with a sort of hopelessness," and during coal strikes they "squat in silent remoteness" on the hills above the roads leading down to the mines, watching the "blue-bottles," the police, who watch back. They have changed because they've got a "new kind of shallow consciousness, all newspaper and cinema," and yet underneath they feel a "heaviness," a loss of life ("Bestwood," 264).

Nowhere does Lawrence describe this collapse of instinctive trust in life more vividly than in chapter 11 of *Lady Chatterley's Lover.* "England, My England! But which is *my* England?" the chapter asks. The England of old, with its agriculture and wild village nights, or the new, with its brittle little mining villages, its big cities, and nervous pursuits? "The younger generation were utterly unconscious of the old England. There was a gap in the continuity of consciousness, almost American: but industrial really. What next?" (*LCL,* 170). As Connie takes her car trip through Tevershall, we see a whole town stripped of its self-assurance: "The car ploughed uphill through the long squalid straggle of Tevershall, the blackened brick dwellings, the black slate roofs glistening their sharp edges, the mud black with coal-dust, the pavements wet and black. It was as if dismalness had soaked through and through everything. The utter negation of natural beauty, the utter negation of the gladness of life . . . the England of today . . . was producing a new race of mankind, over-conscious in the money and social and political side, on the spontaneous, intuitive side dead, but dead" (*LCL,* 162–64). Yet despite the ugliness and money grubbing, Lawrence writes in "Return to Bestwood," the answer is to find oneself being driven back "to search one's own soul, for a way out into a new destiny" ("Bestwood," 264).

> For God's sake, let us be men
> not monkeys minding machines
> or sitting with our tails curled
> while the machine amuses us, the radio or film or
>   gramophone.
> Monkeys with a bland grin on our faces.
> ("Let Us Be Men," *Complete Poems,* 450)

Lawrence is well aware of the need for money, of the problems surrounding property ownership, and of the conflict between socialism and capitalism. What he is saying is that in order for men not to become monkeys climbing around in their old cages of despair over war, "the human condition," money, and self-importance, men should, instead, struggle toward a new conception of what it means to be alive, to make it real, and have the courage to destroy their old ideas. What men should live for is "life and the beauty of aliveness, imagination, awareness, and contact" ("Bestwood," 266), things not very new to men. What *would* be new would be for them *to act* on these ideas. And that would be the instinctive trust in life. "Let me find a few men," said Lawrence in his essay "The Reality of Peace," "who are distinct and at ease in themselves like stars. Let me derive no more from the body of mankind. Let me derive direct from life or direct from death, according to the impulse that is in me."[2]

Connie Chatterley is also fleeing from this collapse, and that's why in chapter 12, in a scene to counter the Tevershall sequence, she goes "directly" into the woods, where primroses are "broad, and full of pale abandon," where "columbines were unfolding their ink-purple riches," where everywhere there were "bud-knots and the leap of life!" (*LCL*, 177). In the love scene that follows, the acquisitive ego in both Connie and Mellors is put to rest, and feelings of stillness are described as important—both of these Lawrentian concepts bear more discussion.

The Acquisitive Ego   In the letter Mellors writes to Connie at the end of *Lady Chatterley's Lover,* there is an interesting comment on spending:

> The young ones get mad because they've no money to spend. Their whole life depends on spending money, and now they've got none to spend. That's our civilization and our education: bring up the masses to depend entirely on spending money, and then the money gives out. The pits are working two days, two-and-a-half days a week. . . . It means a man bringing up a family on twenty-five and thirty shillings. The women are the

maddest of all. But then they're the maddest for spending, nowadays.

If you could only tell them that living and spending isn't the
same thing! (*LCL*, 325–26)

Part of Lawrence's definition of the "acquisitive ego" certainly revolves
around the idea that modern people do equate living with spending,
that money is used to satisfy an interior psychological agenda as well as
to buy food. Lawrence's poems and stories often illustrate the surface
behavior of acquisition (see, for instance, his poems "Money/
Madness," "Kill Money," "New Houses, New Clothes," "Don't," and
"The Root of Our Evil" and his story "Things"). Yet there is a deeper
part of Lawrence's definition of acquisition that we need to understand to see how Connie and Mellors defeat it as it plays out its role in
their love.

"Ultimately, we are all busy buying and selling one another"
Lawrence says in his poem "The Root of Our Evil" (*Collected Poems,*
482). This buying and selling characterizes many aspects of our lives:
what we do to get our wages, how we get our jobs, how we collect
things, how industry uses the "labor market, and so forth. But
Lawrence is even more interested in describing the buying and selling
of egos in love, what he calls the "grand complex of helpless acquisitiveness" (*JTLJ*, 106). Underneath our search for more money and our
buying of an endless stream of things, either on credit or in planned
buying, there is what we might call the helpless autoeroticism of continual consumption. This behavior is Lawrence's "grand complex" in
the acquisitive ego.

Connie thinks to herself: modern women were "half-insane to
'get' a man in the same sense that they were half-insane to get a new
gown or set of furs" (*JTLJ*, 105). They seek "power" and "enlargement" of themselves; their acquisitive egos shut off the "strange, tender flow of sex" (*JTLJ*, 105), in order to abstract and cancel a living
relation and thereby turn the male into an object to be consumed. The
woman gets a man in the same sense that she gets a dress, because the
psychological mechanism operating in modern consumption converts
the object into the idea of connection; what is satisfied is the will and

ego of the purchaser. "Leather couch, phonograph, bric-a-brac, [men], jade ashtrays: it is the idea of a relation that is signified in these objects," 'consumed' in them, and consequently annulled as a lived relation."[3] It is, as Connie says, "sheer acquisitive greed and self-seeking," and what Lawrence calls the "lust of self-importance" (*JTLJ*, 105–6). And the men? About them Connie felt the same: what men wanted was to "get the better of a woman, in the sexual inter-course . . . to extend his ego over a woman," to cover her up with it and turn her, too, into a consumable object to get a "sense of self-aggrandizement" in the purchase (*JTLJ*, 105).

The "grand complex of helpless acquisition," Lawrence says, possesses almost all of us in "every class of society on every nation on earth." He calls it a "disease," and he says that it presents symptoms of a "horrible clawing attempt to get some victim into the clutches" of its "egoistic love" (*JTLJ*, 106). And he says that in men, the disease of the acquisitive ego kills off their powers to connect to one another or to women, rendering them dead emotionally, easy victims to predatory groups looking for conformists or to predatory women. Connie says that this disease of acquisition in women between the ages of 40 and 60 renders them "hyaenas," whose "lust was to acquire a new grip over some man" (*JTLJ*, 105). As for adolescents, Lawrence is pessimistic about them, too: "money-getting and love, are a special form of mania. . . . A good deal of this is vaguely felt, by the young: or by some of them. They are paralyzed by fear of a maniacal society, into which they have to grow up. The rest are possessed by the mania, and are maniacs of love and success, pure and simple: success being money, and love being something very close akin" (*JTLJ*, 107). In Connie and Mellors's world, our world, all of us are manic pursuers of money and love, submitting to the demands of our acquisitive egos "in the primal precincts of consumerism."[4]

At the end of chapter 12 in *Lady Chatterley's Lover*, Lawrence illustrates the helpless need of the ego to ask questions and acquire knowledge even immediately after the suspension of the assertive will in sexual fulfillment. Following what is arguably the most detailed and beautiful description of sexual fulfillment for Connie in the novel, we hear her panic, as the awareness of the "outside" world of consumption reemerges in her mind. In the following scene, Lawrence uses the vocabulary of soft mania to describe the reemergence of the acquisitive ego. The clinging, clutching, and gripping of consumption returns. The assertive verbs of the ego are now a counterforce to the objectives of its previous surrender.

"Where are you? Speak to me! Say something to me!" [The reiteration of the "me" with its *idea* of relation.]

He kissed her softly, murmuring: "Ay, my lass!"

But she did not know what he meant, she did not know where he was. In his silence he seemed lost to her. ["Where is the love-object now in my field of compulsive consumption?"]

"You love me, don't you?" she murmured. [The assertive need for acquiring knowledge about the object, as opposed to when her "whole self" had just "quivered unconscious and alive, like plasm" (*LCL*, 188).]

"Ay, tha knows!" he said.

"But tell me!" she pleaded. [Ego pleading in a dangerous and critical world for an abstract summary of their happiness.]

"Ay! Ay! 'ain't ter felt it?" he said dimly, but softly and surely. And she clung close to him . . . [Her love-object de-objectifies himself by asking her if she *felt* his love in her body.]

"You do love me!" she whispered, *assertive*. And his hands stroked her softly . . . still there haunted her *a restless necessity to get a grip on love*. [The full emergence of the acquisitive ego in Lawrence's "grand complex of helpless acquisitiveness," as love is now hoped to be, after all, that consumable object to be possessed through the interrogative.]

"Say you'll always love me!" she pleaded.

"Ay!" he said, abstractedly. And she felt her questions driving him away from her. [In the demand for love is the purchase of its ideal; his reality is driven away by the autopsy of the real; he fades under the alien probe, giving to the dialogue the following confrontation: body versus effaced object.]

. . . there was a warm, half-sleepy remoteness in his beauty that made her want to cry out and *clutch* him, to *have* him. She would never have him . . .

"I love thee that I can go into thee," he said.

"Do you like *me*?" she said, her heart beating.

"It heals it all up, that I can go into thee. I love thee that tha opened to me. *I love thee that I came into thee* like that." [Mellors reemerges as real, as a body instead of the effaced object of purchase; he hopes to put Connie to rest in her body, in his; he cannot love the clutching mental me of her, he loves the opened her, the *stillness* of them both.] (*LCL*, 188–90; emphasis added)

Feelings of "Stillness"

To keep still, and let the wreckage of ourselves go.
—"Be Still!" *Collected Poems*, 514

All through the novel, Lawrence is opposing the idea of natural stillness to the manic activity of purchasing love. Connie flees to the wood in chapter 12 to find relief from her experience of Tevershall in chapter 11, that emblematic town "producing a new race of mankind, over-conscious in the money and social and political side" but dead on the "spontaneous, intuitive side" (*LCL*, 164). In the wood, Connie finds a place where everything is serene, organic, intuitive, a place wholly different from the grey and modern Tevershall. We enter the forest with her and come upon a carefully detailed scene: the cottage standing in the sun, double daffodils rising "in tufts," daisies bordering a path, a "wide-open" door, Mellors eating at the table, "dutch oven before the fire," a "black potato-saucepan" on the hearth, a "blue mug with beer" on the "white oil-cloth," the fire red and low. She greets Mellors and sits down on a "wooden chair, in the sunlight by the door" (*LCL*, 177–78). As in a painting with carefully chosen colors and visual lines, our eyes are pulled in to this scene by following a perspective that patiently and slowly leads us from a foreground of creative nature to an interior that is serene, peaceful, not in the least manic. "How lovely it was here, so *still*," Connie thinks. "Such a beautiful *stillness*, everything alive and *still*," she says to Mellors (*LCL*, 178). Once Lawrence has pulled us into this stillness, however, we are reminded that it is not the stillness of stock happiness or the now clichéd reiterations of the romantic pastoral poem. Lawrence's stillness initiates confrontation between Connie and Mellors, argument, new knowledge. Both Connie and Mellors know that a new direction is being offered to them, and so they fight it out in order to discover that direction. Chapter 12 moves immediately into Mellors's bitterness and anger over what he sees as Connie using him "to get a child" (*LCL,* 181).

> "That was why you wanted me then, to get a child?" She hung her head.
>   "No. Not really," she said.
>   "What then, *really?*" he asked rather bitingly.
>   She looked up at him reproachfully, saying: "I don't know." He broke into a laugh.
>   "Then I'm damned if I do," he said. (*LCL,* 181)

With that Connie goes back home, admits to herself that she had made use of him, and then quickly decides to return to the hut. When they make love, as discussed earlier, Connie discovers how "cold and derisive her queer female mind stood apart" from the love, looking down on what she saw as the ridiculous butting "haunches" of the man (*LCL,* 184–85). Why does Lawrence plant conflict in the soil of stillness? To show us how firmly we resist our fulfillment. We "resist our own fulfillment with a perseverance that would almost stop the sun in its course," Lawrence says in "The Reality of Peace" (669). "But in the end we are overborne." In the very next scene: it "was from herself" that Connie wanted to be saved, "from her own inward anger and resistance. Yet how powerful was that inward resistance that possessed her!" When she makes love for the second time, "the resistance was gone, and she began to melt in a marvelous peace" (*LCL,* 186). Both Connie and Mellors resist yet give in to being carried away by the "rarest prompting." They "abide by the incalculable impulse of creation," they "lapse upon a current" that carries them "like repose, and extinguishes in repose" their manic selves and wounded wills. They yield up their wills to an unknown. "When we have become very *still,*" Lawrence says, "when there is an inner silence as complete as death, then . . . we hear the rare, superfine whispering of the new direction; the *intelligence* comes" ("Peace," 670–71; emphasis added). And when she touches Mellors now, he feels not repellent, as before, but strangely beautiful, for there is in this stillness she feels the desire for both creation and dissolution, the desire for the impulse of creation, and the desire for destruction in new knowledge. She no longer feels the "weary need of our day to *exert* herself in love."[5]

> How lovely, how lovely, strong, and yet pure and delicate, such *stillness* of the sensitive body! Such utter *stillness* of potency and delicate flesh! . . . And out of *his* utter, *incomprehensible stillness,* she felt again the slow, momentous, surging rise of the phallus again, the other power. . . .
>
> And this time *his* being within her was all soft and iridescent . . . such as no consciousness could seize. Her whole self quivered unconscious and alive, like plasm . . . And afterwards *she* was utterly *still* . . . And *he* was *still* with her. . . . And of this, they would never speak. (*LCL,* 188; emphasis added)

What is this new peace, then, that both Connie and Mellors feel, this "true freedom of peace"? It is both the "pain of being destroyed in all our old securities that we used to call peace" and joy in the "inward suggestion of fulfillment" ("Peace," 670). It is the *intelligence* in the body's experience that says: this body is now felt as body, not market product. And exactly what is this *stillness?* It is not the hard-edged, rapid compulsion of our mental pursuit of "happiness." It is the choice to let the "wreckage of ourselves go," the choice to submerge in the strange and hostile, slightly repulsive unknown. This choice will quiet the acquisitive ego, subvert the autoeroticism of manic consumption, and undermine our "grand complex of helpless acquisition."

Final Plea   Lawrence said that his novel was really a study that contrasted the mental conscious with the phallic consciousness. We see this contrast clearly in chapter 12. As discussed previously, Connie begins to question Mellors's love. But his only response is that he loves her because he "came into" her the way he did, and the way she let him. Then his explanations get specific, so that the phallic consciousness can be defined, and he is as tender as he can be with his use of those words our modern world uses in anger and spite. "Cunt," he says, is Connie "down there," and what he gets when he is inside her and what she gets when he is inside her.

"Cunt! It's like fuck then" Connie says.

"Nay nay! Fuck's only what you do. Animals fuck. But cunt's a lot more than that. It's thee, dost see: an' tha'rt a lot beside an animal, aren't ter? Even ter fuck! Cunt! Eh, that's the beauty o' thee, lass!"

She got up and kissed him between the eyes, that looked at her so dark and soft and unspeakably warm, so unbearably beautiful.

"Is it?" she said. "And do you care for me?"

He kissed her without answering.

"Tha mun goo, let me dust thee," he said.

His hand passed over the curves of her body, firmly, without desire, but with soft, intimate knowledge.

As she ran home in the twilight the world seemed a dream; the trees in the park seemed bulging and surging at anchor on a tide, and the heave of the slope to the house was alive. (*LCL*, 191)

What Mellors tries to say here, and why to Connie the trees seemed to bulge and surge, Lawrence explains this way:

Like the waters of the Red Sea, the blood is divided in a dual polarity between the sexes. As the night falls and the consciousness sinks deeper, suddenly the blood is heard hoarsely calling. Suddenly the deep centres of the sexual consciousness rouse to their spontaneous activity. Suddenly there is a deep circuit established between me and the woman. Suddenly the sea of blood which is me heaves and rushes towards the sea of blood which is her. There is a moment of pure frictional crisis and contact of blood. And then all the blood in me ebbs back into its ways, transmuted, changed. And this is the profound basis of my renewal, my deep blood renewal.

And this has nothing to do with pretty faces or white skin or rosy breasts or any of the rest of the trappings of sexual love. These trappings belong to the day. Neither eyes nor hands nor mouth have anything to do with the final massive and dark collision of the blood in the sex crisis, when the strange flash of electric transmutation passes through the blood of the man and the blood of the woman. They fall apart and sleep in their transmutation. (*Unconscious,* 202–3)

The bomb Lawrence throws at the skull of idealism in chapter 12 is the distinction he makes between "fucking" (what we do and think about), and "cunt" (what we feel). The blood knowledge of our bodies is based on the acceptance of the man's body by the woman and of the woman's body by the man. For Lawrence firmly believed that men and women are not fundamentally at odds with each other. All living things, especially human beings, for Lawrence, are in active relation with one another, whether they know it or not, and when that living relation is broken or torn apart, as it sometimes is when men put machines between themselves and nature, or when men put their personalties between themselves and the women they love, then, Lawrence says, men fail to live. Blood consciousness with nature, and between the maleness and femaleness in men and women, is our salvation from what Lawrence calls our "iron world."

Trees, for example, give out life, Lawrence said in his essay "Pan in America," "as I give out life. Our two lives meet and cross one another, unknowingly: the tree's life penetrates my life, and my life the tree's . . . It vibrates its presence into my soul . . . I think no man could live near a pine tree and remain quite suave and supple and compliant. Something fierce and bristling is communicated."[6] It is the same for men and women. The fierce and bristling nature of our individualities is needed as we connect with each other tenderly and in unison. For without the "night-consummation we are trees without roots." "Sex then is a polarization of the individual blood in man towards the individual blood in woman" (*Unconscious,* 212). For Lawrence, this polarization does not emanate from the "whole rank tangle of liberated, degenerate feelings," products of Freud's analysis of our tamed, civilized, and repressed lives ("Feelings," 758–59). It emanates from our deeper lost feelings, the "honourable beasts of our being, whose voice echoes wordless and for ever wordless down the darkest avenues of the soul." We have to struggle with the "old Jewish horror of the true

Adam," the mysterious "primeval place in man, where God is, if He is anywhere." We have to educate ourselves by listening, "listening-in to the voices of the honourable beasts that call in the dark paths of the veins of our body, from the God in the heart . . . not for words nor for inspiration, but to the lowing of the innermost beasts, the feelings, that roam in the forests of the blood" ("Feelings," 759). And when and if we do hear this beast, we realize it is our own solitary self, our own blood, our senses' tender, that final plea from our bodies not to turn our backs on life. Even when our desires are dead, the beasts wait, wait for changes, as Lawrence explains in the poem "Desire is Dead":

> Desire may be dead
> and still a man can be
> a meeting place for sun and rain,
> wonder outwaiting pain
> as in a wintry tree
> (*Complete Poems*, 504)

And when our desires are alive, demanding change, we might say to someone, as we "catch flesh like the night" in our arms ("After Dark," *Complete Poems*, 428):

> You, you don't know me
> When have your knees ever nipped me
> like fire-tongs a live coal
> for a minute?
> ("You," *Complete Poems*, 427)

But can we listen to our own blood demands? Can we afford to let our senses' tender stage their final plea? To request our full acceptance of the body? We might try, as Connie and Mellors have tried. But if we can't, for whatever reasons, good or bad, then we can at least "look in the real novels," like *Women in Love* or *Lady Chatterley's Lover*, and there hear the "low, calling cries of the characters" whose wonder outwaits their pain. Mellors's wonder finds the courage to accept Connie's vagina, gaining knowledge of the womb and the phallus; Connie accepts Mellors's penis, gaining knowledge of the phallus and the womb. This hope, this acceptance of each other's essential nature as man and woman, will change Connie and Mellors and change their relationship to their outside worlds, as we shall see in the last chapters of *Lady Chatterley's Lover*.[7]

6

Hope

A man has to fend and fettle for the best, and then trust in something beyond himself. You can't insure against the future, except by really believing in the best bit of you, and in the power beyond it. So I believe in the little flame between us. . . . That's what I abide by, and will abide by, Cliffords and Berthas, colliery companies and governments and the money-mass of people all notwithstanding.
—*Lady Chatterley's Lover*

The conclusion Mellors has reached above was a hard-fought one. It reflects what both Connie and Mellors feel is the answer to the uncompromising world around them. Both have refused to take their plight tragically, as those around them would like them to do. To paraphrase the opening paragraph of this novel: Connie and Mellors have built between them new hopes among the ruins, they have gone around and scrambled over the obstacles, no matter how many skies have fallen. D. H. Lawrence presents a struggle for fulfillment that gives us not tragedy but possibility—even as he attacks romantic love and the marriage of compatibility. Connie and Mellors are characters who, as one critic put it, have "stopped looking for loopholes. They acknowledge life is a struggle and they 'move along.' "[1]

With *Lady Chatterley's Lover* Lawrence simply knocks the wind out of tragedy as high art. No longer does Lawrence dramatize the tragedy of sadism in history or the drama of men and women who rebel against custom and then die in the end. He has looked long enough at tragedy, has understood it, and has tired of it. Tragedy begins to look to him like a man "in love with his own defeat / Which is only a sloppy way of being in love with yourself" ("Tragedy," *Complete Poems,* 508). And so, with *Lady Chatterley's Lover,* Lawrence presents a step-by-step initiation into a new relationship between a man and a woman after the apocalypse of war and exploitive industrialization. It is new because it exposes, and perhaps it provides a solution to, what Virginia Woolf in *To the Lighthouse* said she saw as the main problem between men and women. She said there was this "sterility of the male" that consisted of a plea for sympathy with his failure to live "in the heart of life" and that would often, if not always, kill life in a woman, too.[2] James Joyce's Leopold Bloom makes this kind of a plea throughout *Ulysses,* finally submitting to the response Molly makes to such a request: she will dominate him.

The most striking example of how Lawrence departs from Joyce's and Woolf's description of the failure to live in the heart of life can be found at the end of *John Thomas and Lady Jane* where, as in the scene that follows, sexual experience is still found in the midst of forces that try to prevent it. At the end of her novel *Between the Acts,* Woolf announces with a great sigh of despair and spite that we all must be John Thomases and Lady Janes, full of tragic feelings in a brutal world (*Acts,* 190, 199–200). Joyce, at the end of *Ulysses,* turns his back on the idea of fulfilling sex between men and women and gives the last chapter over to the Sheela-na-gig, that mythical, emasculating figure in Irish folklore.[3] By the end of *John Thomas and Lady Jane,* even though Connie and Parkin (who becomes Mellors in *Lady Chatterley's Lover*) have lost touch with what they had gained earlier in the novel (that tender awareness of life, free from what Lawrence called the "frictional, seething, resistant, explosive, blind sort" of modern energy in themselves), they have learned that their awareness can at times carry them through their days in an "iron world." The two take a footpath down into a little hollow of a wood. It is Sunday, and they are suddenly surrounded by churchgoers, miners and their families, and lords and ladies.

> He looked up, and saw a keeper, a big-faced, middle-aged man, striding round the brambles and dog-rose thickets. Quickly he put down her dress, and as she began to lift her face he murmured:
> "Keep still! There's keeper! Dunna move!" And he held her closer.
> "Now then!" said the burly keeper, in ugly challenge, and Parkin felt all her body jolt in his arms. He pressed her closer. The keeper was smiling an ugly smile.
> "Let us be, man, can't you!" said Parkin, in a soft, quiet voice, looking into the light-blue, half-triumphant eyes of the other fellow. "We're harmin' nothing. Have yer niver 'ad a woman in your arms yourself!" The perfect quiet rebuke of his voice was in key with the steady, unabashed rebuke in his eyes. (*JTLJ*, 374)

Connie does not jump up and run off, and Parkin does not feel embarrassed. The "unabashed rebuke" in Parkin's voice and eyes undermines the interloper's attempted rebuke, and he leaves them alone. Parkin's rebuke defeats our own attempts to see this scene as tragic melodrama because it carries no plea for sympathy as a failure to live "in the heart of life." It is the strong, powerful rebuke of life, and Connie's reaction in the presence of such life is to be suddenly and involuntarily encouraged:

> "Kiss me!" she whispered. "Kiss me.—I know the old squire here—."
> He kissed her many times, she was so queer and sightless. (*JTLJ*, 375)

"Queer and sightless" behavior is what Lawrence calls sexuality in *Lady Chatterley's Lover*. It is what Connie and Mellors learn, at the end of the novel, that they want. What "liars poets and everybody were! They made one think one wanted sentiment. When what one supremely wanted was this piercing, consuming, rather awful sensuality. To find a man who dared do it, without shame or sin or final mis-giving" (*LCL*, 268). Mellors learns that his feeling, "all mixed up with a lot of rage," is a certain courage of his own tenderness for a woman. He learns that as he went into Connie, the "thing he had to do" was "to come into tender touch, without losing his pride or his dignity or his integrity as a man" (*LCL*, 302). How different this all is from Woolf's conclusion about sex in *Between the Acts* or from Joyce's in *Ulysses*. When Mellors describes at the end of the novel his liking for farming, we find out that until he can purchase a farm of his own he will work on the Butler and Smitham Colliery Company farm, which provides hay and oats for pit-ponies. "I like farming all right," he says. It's not "inspiring, but then I don't ask to be inspired. I'm used to hors-es, and cows, though they are very female, have a soothing effect on me. When I sit with my head in her side, milking, I feel very solaced" (*LCL*, 325). This is hardly the conventional stature of the Western hero, hardly the popular notion of the tragic hero, with his head pressed against the side of a cow. Lawrence was not interested in the old roles of tragic melodrama or of romance or in roles that would make his characters appear archetypical. His point was to show that if we want to see beyond our conventional beliefs, we must have the courage to drop them.

In chapters 15 to 19, then, Lawrence describes the attempts of both lovers to free themselves from the social mess their love has made. Both have become incorrigible to all the conventions around them, incorrigible to conventional marriage, to the conventional defi-nitions of love, sex, and compatibility held by society, and incorrigible to English class expectations concerning propriety and money. Connie clearly and straightforwardly denies Clifford's beliefs.

> "Give me the body. I believe the life of the body is a greater reali-ty than the life of the mind: when the body is really wakened to life. But so many people, like your famous wind-machine, have only got minds tacked on to their physical corpses."
>
> ". . . The life of the body," he said, "is just the life of the animals."
>
> "And that's better than the life of professional corpses. But it's not true! The human body is only just coming to real life. With

the Greeks it gave a lovely flicker, then Plato and Aristotle killed it, and Jesus finished it off. But now the body is coming really to life, it is really rising from the tomb. And it will be a lovely, lovely life in the lovely universe, the life of the human body."

"My dear, you speak as if you were ushering it all in! . . . Believe me, whatever God there is is slowly eliminating the guts and alimentary system from the human being, to evolve a higher, more spiritual being."

"Why should I believe you, Clifford, when I feel that whatever God there is has at last wakened up in my guts, as you call them, and is rippling so happily there, like dawn. Why should I believe you, when I feel so very much the contrary?" (*LCL*, 254)

Connie has finally let Clifford have it, as does Mellors with Hilda, a little later:

A man gets a lot of enjoyment out o' that lass theer, which is more than anybody gets out o' th' likes o' you. Which is a pity, for you might 'appen a' bin a good apple, 'stead of a handsome crab. Women like you needs proper graftin'."

He was looking at her with an odd, flickering smile, faintly sensual and appreciative.

"And men like you," she said, "ought to be segregated: justifying their own vulgarity and selfish lust."

"Ay, ma'am! It's a mercy there's a few men left like me. But you deserve what you get: to be left severely alone." (*LCL*, 266)

Sure of their own feelings when confronted by others, Connie and Mellors deliver their blows with simple force and eloquence. "In life," says Wayne Burns, "the rightness of the guts (as against the mind) will depend on one's point of view. In Lawrence's as in all other novels, however, the guts are always right; it is an axiom or principle of the novel that they are always right, that the senses of even a fool can give the lie to even the most profound abstractions of the noblest thinker."[4]

With each other, however, Connie and Mellors are much more complicated—even less confident. In chapter 15, for example, we heard Mellors condemning the middle classes as "ladylike prigs with half a ball" and the working classes as those believing in bolshevism and money worship (*LCL*, 234). His complaint initiated a despair in him, and he calls into question whether he had a right to bring Connie's child into the world. Connie is shocked and announces that he "*can't* even really want" her then. "Tell me you want a child, in hope!" she murmurs to him (*LCL*, 236). He doesn't answer, but continues for a whole page on how he plans to save both bosses and workers from industrial tedium. When Mellors says "the root of sanity is in the balls," Connie gathers his testicles into her hand as he talks more and more about his utopian plans. He is too depressed to respond to her, however. He can't even answer Connie's question: "But don't you care about the future?" This scene is surely a bit of satire, a bit of humor: Connie finds the "root of sanity" in Mellors's balls, not in his understandably angry but half-baked schemes to save the world. Only when Mellors sees Connie throw off her clothes to run out in the rain does he laugh at himself and throw off his clothes, too, to join her, seeing her "rounded buttocks" take flight in nakedness (*LCL*, 239). It was "too much" for him. Oliver Mellors sees hope in Lady Chatterley, and as far as the "future" is concerned, he sees that in the Lady's "soft sloping bottom. . . . It's a bottom as could hold the world up, it is" (*LCL*, 241).

Of course this kind of quasiphilosophy is blasphemous to political idealists, responsible capitalists and socialists, conventional preachers and academics—and Lawrence knew it. In the wood, Connie and Mellors have become creatures. Mellors now makes love to her "short and sharp," like an "animal," and Connie dances naked, her "full loins and buttocks . . . offered in a kind of homage" to Mellors (*LCL*, 239–40), who reaffirms his feelings and discards his despair about bosses and workers: "An' if I only lived ten minutes, an' stroked thy arse an' got to know it, I should reckon I'd lived *one* life, sees ter! Industrial system or not! Here's one o' my lifetimes" (*LCL*, 241).

Later, in chapter 17, even though Connie, too, despairs, after hearing about the details of Bertha's married life with Mellors, she will reaffirm her feelings for him. Despite her craving for "utter respectability" after feeling that Mellors is "really common, really low," and despite her being "terrified of society" and what people will think, she still says to herself: "What had he done, after all? What had he done to herself, Connie, but give her an exquisite pleasure, and a sense of freedom and life? He had released her warm, natural sexual flow. And for that they would hound him down" (*LCL*, 287). As Connie must stick to him, to what she *had of him,* so Mellors must stick to her, to what he *had of her,* whether they get together in the end or not.

This does not happen with Virginia Woolf or James Joyce. Our traditional views about unfulfilled love are upheld, our despair over the conventional tragedy of a loveless world dramatized as inevitable. And so we call their novels "greater," in our conventional criticism, that is, easier to swallow. When we experience the scenes between Connie and Mellors, with their detailed sexual unions, we witness sexual feelings we either do not have and want, have had and lost, or are getting. It is the getting of them that is frightening, more frightening than the losing of them, through which we can take refuge in our conventional sadness, our popular notion of tragedy. This is why the current trend in literary criticism is to "go beyond" Lawrence, for his books, unlike most of our contemporary fiction, hold a dangerous possibility: that sexual fulfillment can be found in a world gone mad with guilt. After looking for every neurosis Lawrence might have suffered from, critics have tried to apply their theories of his neuroses to his novels in such a way as to undermine this real danger. Paul Eggert defines this current trend in Lawrence studies this way: "We most of us live at a duller level of responsiveness, a slower intellectual pace than he—which is no crime; the crime is in portraying Lawrence as having done so as well, portraying him as a toned-down Lawrence who is seen as extending but essentially reinforcing our own pieties about normality and society."[5]

In the intense moments when human beings become creatures, *Lady Chatterley's Lover* finds its greatest importance. And even if Mellors is too preachy about sexual behavior or politics, the book still shows us both Connie and Mellors wrestling to get free from their mental conceptions of the self and from *our* intellectual frameworks called myth, archetype, historical progress, and the marriage of sexual compatibility. Characters in Joyce and Woolf do live and battle with their old ideas on sex and history, but they stay caged in their

Aristotelian concepts about such a fight. Lawrence tried to break that cage, to let out the "tremble of life" in himself, and in us. He was never interested in giving *Lady Chatterley's Lover* a conventional happy ending—the world of this novel is too complex for that. In a Lawrence story, hope is found through inner struggle and individual action. But it is always a hope qualified and complicated by the ramifications of that struggle and action. It won't be a future where the lovers go to Canada, or where promises can be kept about living together forever; rather, it will be a future where individuals learn, despite their "wounds," that they can feel alive again.

Hope for Mellors, then, is more than loving Connie. He tells her that his life must "get somewhere," inwardly at least, before he would live with her. Connie asks him: "What is the point of your existence?" He's not sure, so Connie tells him:

> Shall I tell you what you have that other men don't have, and that will make the future? Shall I tell you?"
> "Tell me then," he replied.
> "It's the courage of your own tenderness, that's what it is.
> (*LCL,* 300)

When they get back to his room in London, Connie appears to be doing most of the teaching about what hope Mellors has in his life now.

> "I've a dread of puttin' children i' th' world," he said. "I've such a dread o' th' future for 'em."
> "But you've put it into me. Be tender to it, and that will be it's future already. Kiss it!" (*LCL,* 302)

When they make love this time, Mellors finally realizes as he goes in to her "that this was the thing he had to do, to come into tender touch, without losing his pride or his dignity or his integrity as a man. After all, if she had money and means, and he had none, he should be too proud and honorable to hold back his tenderness from her on that account. 'I stand for the touch of bodily awareness between human beings,' he said to himself, 'and the touch of tenderness. And she is my mate. And it is a battle against the money, and the machine, and the insentient ideal monkeyishness of the world' " (*LCL,* 302).

Hope for Connie was not only her child and a belief in a future with Mellors, but also her feeling that she will remain profoundly shameless: "Shame, which is fear: the deep organic shame, the old, old physical fear which crouches in the bodily roots of us, and can only be chased away by the sensual fire, at last it was roused up and routed by the phallic hunt of the man, and she came to the very heart of the jungle of herself. She felt, now, she had come to the real bedrock of her nature, and was essentially shameless" (*LCL,* 268).

For D. H. Lawrence, hope lives in his idea that "perhaps one day even the general public will desire to look . . . [at] the creative portrayals of the sexual impulse . . . which are necessary for the fulfillment of our consciousness" ("Pornography," 187). He believed *Lady Chatterley's Lover* was indeed such a creative portrayal. But before we can experience a change in feeling, even after reading such a creative portrayal of the sexual impulse, Lawrence tells us that we must go back "before Plato, before the tragic idea of life arose, to get on to our feet again."

> Back, before the idealist religions and philosophies arose and started man on the great excursion of tragedy. The last three thousand years of mankind have been an excursion into ideals, bodilessness, and tragedy, and now the excursion is over. And it is like the end of a tragedy in the theatre. The stage is strewn with dead bodies, worse still, with meaningless bodies, and the curtain comes down.
>
> But in life, the curtain never comes down on the scene. There the dead bodies lie, and the inert ones, and somebody has to clear them away, somebody has to carry on. It is the day after. Today is already the day after the end of the tragic and idealist epoch. Utmost inertia falls on the remaining protagonists. Yet we have to carry on. ("A Propos," 354–55)

This is Lawrence's hope for us.

Notes

Because the Cambridge University edition of D. H. Lawrence's letters is still in production, all citations to his letters are taken from H. T. Moore's *The Collected Letters of D. H. Lawrence*. When citations cannot be located in the Moore volumes, available volumes in the Cambridge University edition are used.

Preface

1. D. H. Lawrence, "The Novel and the Feelings," in *Phoenix: The Posthumous Papers of D. H. Lawrence*, ed. E. D. McDonald (New York: Viking Penguin Books, 1978), 760; hereafter cited in text as "Feelings."

2. D. H. Lawrence, "Why the Novel Matters," in *Phoenix*, 535–38; hereafter cited in text as "Novel."

3. D. H. Lawrence, letter to Carlo Linati, 22 January 1925, in *The Collected Letters of D. H. Lawrence*, ed. H. T. Moore (New York: Viking Press, 1962), 2:827; hereafter cited in text as *Collected Letters*.

Chapter 1

1. E. M. Forster, *Aspects of the Novel* (New York: Harcourt, Brace, and World, 1927), 9.

2. See A. R. and C. P. Griffin, "A Social and Economic History of Eastwood and the Nottinghamshire Mining Company," in *A D. H. Lawrence Handbook*, ed. Keith Sagar (New York: Barnes and Noble, 1982), 127–63.

3. D. H. Lawrence, "Nottingham and the Mining Countryside," in *Phoenix*, 135–36; hereafter cited in text as "Nottingham."

4. Gerald Lacy, "Lawrence's Life in the Context of World Events," in *A D. H. Lawrence Handbook*, 216–21.

5. D. H. Lawrence, "Return to Bestwood," in *Phoenix II: Uncollected, Unpublished, and Other Prose Works by D. H. Lawrence*, ed. W. Roberts and

H. T. Moore (New York: Viking Press, 1970), 264; hereafter cited in text as "Bestwood."

6. D. H. Lawrence, "Autobiographical Fragment," in *Phoenix,* 817; hereafter cited in text as "Fragment."

7. D. H. Lawrence, "What Is a Man to Do?" in *The Complete Poems of D. H. Lawrence,* ed. Vivian de Sola Pinto and Warren Roberts (New York: Viking Press, 1971), 631–32; all poems quoted in text are from this edition, hereafter cited as *Complete Poems.*

Chapter 2

1. See Lawrence's "We Need One Another," in *Phoenix,* 188–95.

2. Diana Trilling, "Letter to a Young Critic," in *The Selected Letters of D. H. Lawrence,* ed. Diana Trilling (Garden City, N.Y.: Anchor Books, 1961), xxxiii.

3. D. H. Lawrence, "The Two Principles," in *Phoenix II,* 227.

4. D. H. Lawrence, "Love," in *Phoenix,* 154; hereafter cited in text.

5. D. H. Lawrence, *Psychoanalysis and the Unconscious and Fantasia of the Unconscious* (New York: Viking Press, 1960), 203; hereafter cited in text as *Unconscious.*

6. D. H. Lawrence, "The Real Thing," in *Phoenix,* 197.

7. D. H. Lawrence, "Pornography and Obscenity," in *Phoenix,* 177–78; hereafter cited in text as "Pornography."

8. For a complete discussion of Lawrence's legacy along these lines, see Kingsley Widmer's "Lawrence's Cultural Impact," in *The Legacy of D. H. Lawrence* (New York: St. Martin's Press, 1987), 156–74; see J. Meyers's introduction to this volume for an overview of Lawrence's influence on modern writers.

9. Sigmund Freud, "Creative Writers and Day-Dreaming," in *The Freud Reader,* ed. Peter Gay (New York: W. W. Norton and Co., 1989), 443.

10. D. H. Lawrence, *The First Lady Chatterley* (New York: Dial Press, 1944), vi.

11. Wayne Burns, "D. H. Lawrence: The Beginnings of a Primer to the Novel," in *Toward a Contextualist Aesthetic of the Novel* (Seattle: Genitron Press, 1968), 208.

Chapter 3

1. R. P. Draper, *D. H. Lawrence: The Critical Heritage* (New York: Barnes and Noble, 1970), 280; hereafter cited in text.

2. Edmund Wilson, "Signs of Life," *New Republic,* 3 July 1929, 184.

3. W. T. Andrews, *Critics on D. H. Lawrence* (Coral Gables, Fla.: University of Miami Press, 1971), 36; hereafter cited in text.

Notes

4. T. S. Eliot, *After Strange Gods: A Primer of Modern Heresy* (London: Faber and Faber, 1934), 61.

5. Frieda Lawrence, *"Not I, But the Wind . . ."* (Carbondale: Southern Illinois University Press, 1974), 193.

6. Richard Aldington, *D. H. Lawrence: Portrait of a Genius But . . .* (New York: Collier Books, 1950), 302.

7. Mark Spilka, *The Love Ethic of D. H. Lawrence* (Bloomington and London: Indiana University Press, 1955).

8. D. Jackson and F. B. Jackson, eds., *Critical Essays on D. H. Lawrence* (Boston: G. K. Hall and Co., 1988), 9; hereafter cited in text.

9. F. R. Leavis, *D. H. Lawrence: Novelist* (London: Chatto and Windus, 1955), 74.

10. D. H. Lawrence, letter to Witter Bynner, 13 March 1928, in *The Letters of D. H. Lawrence,* ed. James T. Bolton (Cambridge: Cambridge University Press, 1991), 6:321; hereafter cited in text as *Letters.*

11. Keith Sagar, *The Art of D. H. Lawrence* (Cambridge: Cambridge University Press, 1966), 195; hereafter cited in text.

12. See H. M. Daleski, *The Forked Flame: A Study of D. H. Lawrence* (Evanston, Ill.: Northwestern University Press, 1965), 258–311; hereafter cited in text.

13. Wayne Burns, "Lady Chatterley's Lover: A Pilgrim's Progress for Our Time," *Paunch* 26 (1966): 20–21.

14. Wayne Burns, "D. H. Lawrence: The Beginnings of a Primer to the Novel," in *Toward a Contextualist Aesthetic of the Novel* (Seattle: Genitron Press, 1968), 198; hereafter cited in text.

15. Kingsley Widmer, "Notes on the Literary Institutionalization of D. H. Lawrence: An Anti-Review of the Current State of Lawrence Studies," *Paunch* 26 (1966):5.

16. Jackson and Jackson, 23. One essay in C. Heywood's collection, *D. H. Lawrence: New Studies* (London: Macmillan Press, 1987), 104–23, even discusses *Lady Chatterley's Lover* as an example of Lawrence's use of contemporary ganglionic nervous control theories.

17. Scott Sanders, *D. H. Lawrence: The World of the Five Major Novels* (New York: Viking Press, 1973), 205; hereafter cited in text.

18. Michael Squires, *The Creation of Lady Chatterley's Lover* (Baltimore and London: Johns Hopkins University Press, 1983), 185; hereafter cited in text.

19. Peter Scheckner, *Class, Politics and the Individual: A Study of the Major Works of D. H. Lawrence* (Rutherford, N.J.: Fairleigh Dickinson Press, 1985), 159, 168.

20. Mark Spilka, "On Lawrence's Hostility to Wilful Women: The Chatterley Solution," in *Lawrence and Women,* ed. Anne Smith (New York: Barnes and Noble, 1978), 210.

Notes

21. L. L. Martz, "The Second Lady Chatterley," in *The Spirit of D. H. Lawrence,* ed. G. Salgãdo and G. K. Das (Totowa, N.J.: Barnes and Noble, 1988), 120.

22. Anthony Burgess, *Flame into Being: The Life and Work of D. H. Lawrence* (New York: Arbor House, 1985), ix, 237–38.

23. D. H. Lawrence, "Introduction to These Paintings," in *Phoenix,* 570. P. Fjågesund calls Lawrence a "phallic freak" in *The Apocalyptic World of D. H. Lawrence* (Oslo: Norwegian University Press, 1991), 79.

Chapter 4

1. Graham Hough, *The Dark Sun* (New York: Capricorn, 1956), 160–61; John Worthen, *D. H. Lawrence and the Idea of the Novel* (Totowa, N.J.: Rowman and Littlefield, 1979), 177.

2. Julian Moynahan, *"Lady Chatterley's Lover:* The Deed of Life," in *D. H. Lawrence: A Collection of Critical Essays,* ed. M. Spilka (Englewood Cliffs, N.J.: Prentice-Hall, 1963), 86.

3. Lydia Blanchard, "Lawrence, Foucault, and the Language of Sexuality," in *D. H. Lawrence's "Lady": A New Look at Lady Chatterley's Lover* ed. M. Squires and D. Jackson (Athens: University of Georgia Press, 1985), 31.

4. D. H. Lawrence, *John Thomas and Lady Jane* (New York: Penguin Books, 1977), 105; hereafter cited in text as *JTLJ.*

5. Virginia Woolf, *Between the Acts* (New York: Harcourt, Brace, Jovanovich, 1969), 14; hereafter cited in text as *Acts.*

6. David Parker, "Lawrence and Lady Chatterley: The Teller and the Tale," *Critical Review* 20 (1978): 31–41. Parker explores the difference between the third and first drafts of the novel, seeing that difference as one of "unconscious delicacy" and "writing unidealized" (38, 34).

7. C. L. Ross, "Introduction," *Women in Love* (New York: Penguin Books, 1986), 27.

8. D. H. Lawrence, "Foreword to Women in Love," in *Phoenix II,* 275–76.

9. D. H. Lawrence, *Women in Love* (New York: Penguin Books, 1986), 295; hereafter cited in text as *WIL.*

10. Robert Scholes, *Semiotics and Interpretation* (New Haven, Conn.: Yale University Press, 1982), 140.

11. Mark Spilka, "Lawrence and the Clitoris," in *The Challenge of D. H. Lawrence,* ed. Michael Squires and Keith Cushman (Madison: University of Wisconsin Press, 1990), 183.

12. H. T. Moore, *The Intelligent Heart: The Story of D. H. Lawrence* (New York: Farrar, Straus and Young, 1954), 219.

13. D. H. Lawrence, "Fenimore Cooper's Leatherstocking Novels," in *Studies in Classic American Literature* (New York: Penguin Books, 1977), 66; hereafter cited in text as "Leatherstocking Novels."

14. James Fenimore Cooper, *The Deerslayer* (New York: Signet, 1980), 150–51; hereafter cited in text as *Deerslayer*.

15. See B. D. Lewin, "Sleep, the Mouth, and the Dream Screen," *Psychoanalytic Quarterly* 15 (1946): 419–34.

16. Jean Baudrillard, *Seduction* (New York: St. Martin's Press, 1990), 47; hereafter cited in text.

17. A. Efron, "The Way Our Sympathy Flows and Recoils: Lawrence's Last Theory of the Novel," *Paunch* 63–64 (1990): 75.

18. Wilhelm Reich, *Listen Little Man!* (New York: Farrar, Straus and Giroux, 1948), 53.

19. D. H. Lawrence, "Love Was Once a Little Boy," in *Phoenix II*, 449; hereafter cited in text as "Little Boy."

20. The discussion on Joyce and Woolf is adapted from my "D. H. Lawrence's Answer to the Nightmare of History in Joyce and Woolf," *Liberal and Fine Arts Review* 5, no. 1 (January 1985): 43–54.

21. D. H. Lawrence, "Morality and the Novel," *Selected Literary Criticism*, ed. A. Beal (New York: Viking Press, 1966), 113.

22. James Joyce, *Ulysses* (New York: Random House, 1961), 782.

23. For further discussion, see my *Senses' Tender: Recovering the Novel for the Reader* (New York: Peter Lang, 1989); Gerald J. Butler, *Love and Reading* (New York: Peter Lang, 1989); the journal *Paunch,* issue 63–64 ("New Studies in D. H. Lawrence"), ed. Arthur Efron; and the following by Wayne Burns: "On Reading Novels: An Outline for a Contextualist Primer," *Recovering Literature* 10 (1982): 33–41; *Journey through the Dark Woods* (Seattle: Howe Street Press, 1982); and "Reaffirming the Panzaic," *Recovering Literature* 18, no. 2 (1992): 9–37.

24. Stephen Spender, "D. H. Lawrence, England, and the War," in *D. H. Lawrence: Novelist, Poet, Prophet*, ed. Stephen Spender (London: Weidenfeld and Nicolson, 1973), 76.

Chapter 5

1. Carol Dix, *D. H. Lawrence and Women* (Totowa, N.J.: Rowman and Littlefield, 1980), 88–89.

2. D. H. Lawrence, "The Reality of Peace," in *Phoenix,* 687; hereafter cited in text as "Peace."

3. Jean Baudrillard, "The System of Objects," in his *Selected Writings* (Stanford, Calif.: Stanford University Press, 1988), 24.

Notes

4. L. A. Rickels, *The Case of California* (Baltimore: Johns Hopkins University Press, 1991), 181.

5. D. H. Lawrence, "The Fox," in his *Four Short Novels* (New York: Penguin Books, 1977), 175.

6. D. H. Lawrence, "Pan in America," in *Phoenix,* 25.

7. In another context it may be argued that *Lady Chatterly's Lover* is a response to what Krober and Krober call the "disappearing body in the hype-modern condition." *Body Invaders: Panic Sex in America* (New York: St. Marten's Press, 1987), 20–33.

Chapter 6

1. Duane Edwards, "D. H. Lawrence: Tragedy in the Modern Age," *Literary Review* 24 (1979): 71–88.

2. Virginia Woolf, *To the Lighthouse* (New York: Harcourt, Brace and World, 1927), 58–59.

3. William K. Buckley, "A Dissident's Note on Joyce's Molly Bloom," *North Dakota Quarterly* 51 (Fall 1983): 80–86.

4. Wayne Burns, "The Panzaic Principle," in *Recovering Literature 5,* no. 1 (Spring 1976): 3–63. Reprinted in W. K. Buckley, *Senses' Tender* (New York: Peter Lang, 1989), 105–46.

5. Paul Eggert, "Lawrence Criticism: Where Next?" *Critical Review* 21 (1979): 72–84.

Selected Bibliography

Definitive editions of all of D. H. Lawrence's works are being prepared by Cambridge University Press.

Primary Works

The Collected Letters of D. H. Lawrence. 2 vols. Edited by H. T. Moore. New York: Viking Press, 1962.

The Complete Poems of D. H. Lawrence. Edited by Vivian de Sola Pinto and Warren Roberts. New York: Viking Press, 1964. The first attempt to provide a reliable text for all of Lawrence's poetry.

The First Lady Chatterley. New York: Dial Press, 1944. The first version of *Lady Chatterley's Lover,* with an introduction by Frieda Lawrence, was published in the United States in 1944. It is now available in a British edition published by Heinemann in 1972.

John Thomas and Lady Jane. New York: Penguin Books, 1977. This is the second version of *Lady Chatterley's Lover,* first published in 1954 in Italy. It is a complete novel and contains some interesting passages Lawrence deleted from the third and final version.

Lady Chatterley's Lover. New York: Bantam Books, 1968. This text is the complete and unexpurgated 1928 Orioli edition, and it contains Lawrence's important essay "A Propos of *Lady Chatterley's Lover.*"

The Letters of D. H. Lawrence. Edited by James T. Boulton. Cambridge: Cambridge University Press, 1979–1993.

Phoenix: The Posthumous Papers of D. H. Lawrence. Edited by E. D. McDonald. 1936. New York; Viking Penguin Books, 1978. Essential reading for any student of Lawrence. Contains essays on nature, love, art, education, psychology, and many other topics.

Phoenix II: Uncollected, Unpublished, and Other Prose Works by D. H. Lawrence. Edited by W. Roberts and H. T. Moore. 1959. New York: Viking Press, 1970. Like *Phoenix, Phoenix II* is essential reading. Contains autobiographical sketches, essays on art and behavior, reviews, and stories and sketches.

Secondary Works

Biographies and Memoirs

Aldington, Richard. *D. H. Lawrence: Portrait of a Genius But . . .* New York: Collier Books, 1950. Aldington knew Lawrence, and this book is the first attempt to look objectively at his life and work.

Lawrence, Frieda. *"Not I, But the Wind . . ."* Carbondale: Southern Illinois University Press, 1974. This memoir by Lawrence's wife contains interesting insights into his personality and creative imagination.

Moore, H. T. *The Intelligent Heart: The Story of D. H. Lawrence.* New York: Farrar, Straus and Young, 1954. Still one of the best biographies on Lawrence. It is a detailed history of his life and art, with maps and photos. Revised edition issued as *The Priest of Love: A Life of D. H. Lawrence.* Carbondale: Southern Illinois University Press, 1974.

Nehls, Edward. *D. H. Lawrence: A Composite Biography.* 3 vols. Madison: University of Wisconsin Press, 1957–59. Useful introduction to Lawrence's life through the chronological presentation of letters written by Lawrence and his friends.

Worthen, John. *D. H. Lawrence: A Literary Life.* New York: St. Martin's Press, 1989. One in a series of volumes on British and American authors that is not written in the "spirit of traditional biography" but rather aims at tracing the "professional, publishing and social contexts" that shaped Lawrence's writing.

_____. *D. H. Lawrence: The Early Years, 1885–1912.* Cambridge: Cambridge University Press, 1991. First volume in a definitive biography of Lawrence's life.

Literary Criticism

Balbert, Peter. *D. H. Lawrence and the Phallic Imagination.* New York: St. Martin's Press, 1989. Defends Lawrence against what the author sees as "seductive and misleading" feminist criticism.

Selected Bibliography

Britton, Derek. *Lady Chatterley: The Making of a Novel*. London: Unwin Hyman, 1988. A detailed study of Lawrence's three versions of the novel.

Burns, Wayne. "D. H. Lawrence: The Beginnings of a Primer to the Novel," in his *Toward a Contextualist Aesthetic of the Novel*. Seattle: Genitron Press, 1968. Important essay for undergraduates reading Lawrence for the first time.

Clark, Colin. *River of Dissolution*. New York: Barnes and Noble, 1969. This study attempts to counteract the "moralistic interpretation of Lawrence's fiction by looking at how Lawrence calls into question the dichotomies of decadence and growth, purity and degradation, the parochial and demonic."

Daleski, H. M. *The Forked Flame: A Study of D. H. Lawrence*. Evanston, Ill.: Northwestern University Press, 1965. The chapter on *Lady Chatterley's Lover* ("The Return") contains a valuable discussion of Lawrence's language in the novel and an in-depth analysis of the relationship between Connie and Mellors.

Eliot, T. S. *After Strange Gods: A Primer of Modern Heresy*. New York: Harcourt, Brace, and Co., 1934. Contains an attack on *Lady Chatterley's Lover* that unduly influenced critics and librarians.

Forster, E. M. *Aspects of the Novel*. London: Edward Arnold, 1927. A fine British novelist in his own right, Forster called Lawrence the only true prophetic novelist in a chapter titled "Prophecy."

Gertzman, J. A., "Legitimizing *Lady Chatterley's Lover:* The Grove Press Strategy, 1959." *Paunch* 63–64 (December 1990): 1–14. A detailed discussion of the history behind the 4 May 1959 Grove Press publication of the first legal imprint of *Lady Chatterley's Lover*.

Kermode, Frank. *D. H. Lawrence*. New York: Viking Press, 1973. Compact and useful introductory book for first-time readers. The volume describes nearly the whole of Lawrence's life and most of his major fiction and gives adequate summaries of Lawrence's ideas.

Leavis, F. R. *D. H. Lawrence: Novelist*. New York: Alfred A. Knopf, 1955. The first major defense of Lawrence in England by the foremost critic of his day. The intention of the book was to place Lawrence in the "great tradition" of English literature, but it leaves *Lady Chatterley's Lover* out of the discussion.

Sagar, Keith. *The Art of D. H. Lawrence*. Cambridge: Cambridge University Press, 1966. A comprehensive and chronological treatment of Lawrence's major work. The author states that he will concentrate more on "Lawrence's reaction *against* the English realist tradition" that F. R. Leavis supports in his *D. H. Lawrence: Novelist*.

Sanders, Scott. *D. H. Lawrence: The World of the Five Major Novels*. New York: Viking Press, 1973. Sanders discusses Lawrence's major novels—

Sons and Lovers, The Rainbow, Women in Love, The Plumed Serpent, and *Lady Chatterley's Lover*—as illustrations of Lawrence's belief that a fundamental opposition exists between nature and culture.

Smith, Anne, ed. *Lawrence and Women.* New York: Barnes and Noble, 1978. Smith believes that Lawrence is still "an *experience* and not a classic" who "provokes an urgent and personally profound reaction in his readers." Consequently, her volume is an attempt to "understand the experience of the relationship between men and women as Lawrence presents it in his work."

Squires, Michael. *The Creation of Lady Chatterley's Lover.* Baltimore and London: John Hopkins University Press, 1983. A thematic and structural analysis of all three versions of *Lady Chatterley's Lover.*

_____, and Keith Cushman, eds. *The Challenge of D. H. Lawrence.* Madison: University of Wisconsin Press, 1990. This collection of essays is not "largely concerned with rereading or exegesis, but with the challenge of Lawrence's achievements."

_____, and D. Jackson, eds. *D. H. Lawrence's "Lady": A New Look at Lady Chatterley's Lover.* Athens: University of Georgia Press, 1985. A collection of essays that links the novel to modernist ideas, to the novels of other writers, to Lawrence's oeuvre and literary heritage, and to history.

Bibliographies

Gertzman, Jay A. *A Descriptive Bibliography of Lady Chatterley's Lover, with Essays toward a Publishing History of the Novel.* Westport, Conn.: Greenwood Press, 1989. The bibliography describes the publication and distribution history of the novel. The essays describe the various receptions the novel has received.

Roberts, Warren. *A Bibliography of D. H. Lawrence.* London: Rupert Hart-Davis, 1963.

Court Transcript

Hyde, H. Montgomery. *The Lady Chatterley's Lover Trial.* London: Bodley Head, 1990. The complete court transcript of *Regina v. Penguin Books Limited,* including the decision as to why the novel should not be banned.

Index

Index

Index

The Author

William K. Buckley is associate professor of English at Indiana University, Northwest. He has taught at Miami University in Oxford, Ohio, where he received his Ph.D. in English literature, and at San Diego University, where he received his M.A. He is the editor of *Critical Essays on Cline* (1989), coeditor of *A Half-Century of Cline* (1983) and *Beyond Cheering and Bashing: New Perspectives on "The Closing of the American Mind"* (1992), and author of *Senses' Tender: Recovering the Novel for the Reader* (1989). He has published essays on D. H. Lawrence, James Joyce, and Tennyson and has received awards for scholarship and recognition for undergraduate teaching. He is at work on the book *D. H. Lawrence and British Perceptions of the Wild West*.